PROJECT MANAGEMENT
—
AN ARTIFICIAL INTELLIGENT (AI) APPROACH

Kim Hin David HO

PARTRIDGE

Copyright © 2020 by Kim Hin David HO.

Library of Congress Control Number:		2020912062
ISBN:	Hardcover	978-1-5437-5872-6
	Softcover	978-1-5437-5871-9
	eBook	978-1-5437-5873-3

All rights reserved. No part of this book may be used or reproduced by any means, graphic, electronic, or mechanical, including photocopying, recording, taping or by any information storage retrieval system without the written permission of the author except in the case of brief quotations embodied in critical articles and reviews.

Because of the dynamic nature of the Internet, any web addresses or links contained in this book may have changed since publication and may no longer be valid. The views expressed in this work are solely those of the author and do not necessarily reflect the views of the publisher, and the publisher hereby disclaims any responsibility for them.

Print information available on the last page.

To order additional copies of this book, contact
Toll Free 800 101 2657 (Singapore)
Toll Free 1 800 81 7340 (Malaysia)
orders.singapore@partridgepublishing.com

www.partridgepublishing.com/singapore

CONTENTS

Preface vii

Acknowledgements ix

About the Author xi

Introduction xiii

Chapter 1   Estimating Construction Demand in Singapore: Potential of Neural Networks 1

Chapter 2   Artificial-Intelligence Modelling (AIM) of Hong Kong Real Estate—Principles and Concepts 27

Chapter 3   Energy Resiliency and Sustainability Assessment—Principles and Practical Considerations ... 40

Chapter 4   A Fuzzy Discounted Cash Flow Analysis for the Real Estate Investment Project 49

Chapter 5   Examining Fuzzy Tactical Asset Allocation (FTAA) as an Alternative to Modern Portfolio Theory (MPT) Asset Allocation for International and Direct Real Estate Investment 71

Chapter 6   A Novel Approach of Designing the Knowledge-Based Urban Development (KBUD) adopting the Agent-Based Model (ABM) 106

Chapter 7   The Conclusion 189

Endnotes 197

PREFACE

Over 100 years ago, this was a mud-flat, swamp. Today, this is a modern city. Ten years from now, this will be a metropolis. Never fear.

—the first prime minister of
Singapore, Lee Kuan Yew, 1965

This modern project management (MPM) book is a unique and novel treatment of project management from artificial intelligence (AI) that entails data analytics, deploying neural networks, fuzzy logic, and genetic algorithm(s); and data visualisation, deploying agent-based modelling (ABM) in, for example, the knowledge-based urban development (KBUD). AI is a technology that replicates activities that would normally require human involvement. We have deployed macros in Excel to automate our daily repetitive tasks. We can treat it as the simplest example of AI. Similarly, we did use AI technology in our day-to-day tasks as in modern project management. Unlike before, organisations are now deploying project managers as facilitative leaders rather than directive managers. Such deployment puts more of the decision-making on the team and empowers them to deliver results faster. AI can help project managers transition to facilitative leaders by taking over routine tasks like performance reporting.

The potential impact AI will have on MPM and business can be enormous, to enable them to be nimble. Yet AI is purely dependent on precise and reliable data in and data out. Thus, we need the human input of the project manager to rectify or provide the data. The argument for MPM from an AI approach lies not so much with cost efficiency and effectiveness but primarily with urban sustainability. There is growing support for the argument that when MPM is competently and properly conducted, it adds substantially to the project real estate value, the rental yields, and the sustainable and comfortable built environment.

This MPM book discusses the discipline of project management in modern light and how it can be competently adopted by design engineers, urban planners, project managers, quantity and real estate surveyors, public and private real estate developers, architects for both new and existing developments, as well as scholars.

Happy reading.

Yours sincerely,

Professor Ho, Kim Hin / David
Singapore
August 2020

ACKNOWLEDGEMENTS

The author wishes to extend his most sincere appreciation to the School of Design and Environment, under the highly able deanship of the provost and chair Professor Lam, Khee Poh, of the National University of Singapore. The same wish is extended to the University of Hertfordshire in Hatfield, UK. These two tertiary institutions of higher learning and research are the globally leading universities, inspiring and encouraging both modern and contemporary project management.

ABOUT THE AUTHOR

Dr Ho Kim Hin / David is honorary professor in development economics and land economy, awarded by the UK public university, the University of Hertfordshire. He retired end of May 2019 as professor (associate) (tenured) f/9/9rom the National University of Singapore. Professor Ho spent the last thirty-one years across several sectors, which include the military, oil refining, aerospace engineering, public housing, resettlement, land acquisition, land reclamation, real estate investment, development, and international real estate investing. He spent six years in the real estate career as part of the executive management group of Singapore Technologies at Pidemco Land Limited and as part of the senior management team of the Government of Singapore Investment Corporation's GIC Real Estate Private Limited. Seventeen years have been spent in the National University of Singapore at the then School of Building and Estate Management, the Department of Real Estate, School of Design and Environment, where his research expertise is in two areas. First is international real estate in the area of risk-return behaviour behind international real estate investing in direct and indirect real estate. Second is urban and public policy analysis involving real estate, sea transport, public housing, land, and land use. Schooled in development economics and in land economy at the University of Cambridge, England, he has effectively extended these disciplines to examine his two expertise areas. Apart from being well versed in econometrics, his quantitative interests include real estate demand and supply, investment and finance, artificial intelligent modelling in real estate, and system dynamics modelling for real estate market analysis and public policy analysis. He is a member of the Royal Economics Society (UK), academic member of the National Council of Real Estate Investment Fiduciaries (U.S.), fellow of the American Real Estate Society (U.S.), member of the American Economic Association (U.S.), and member of the Economic Society of Singapore and the Singapore Institute of Management. He holds the degrees of master of philosophy (first class honours with distinction), honorary doctor of letters, and the doctor of philosophy from the University of Cambridge, UK. He has published widely in top international journals and conferences and in chapters of international academic book publishers. Dr Ho has written seven major books (including this book) and undertaken many consultancies and funded research projects. He has written a total of about 275 published works (with ninety-one in peer-reviewed, reputable international journals). He is an editorial board member of the *Journal of Economics and Public Finance, Real Estate Economics* journal, *Journal of Property Research, Journal of Property Investment and Finance, Journal of Real Estate Finance and Economics,* the *Property Management* journal, and the *International Journal of Strategic Property Management.* He has published widely in conferences, finance, chapters of international academic book publishers, undertaken many consultancies, and funded research projects. He is an immediate past governor of the St Gabriel's Foundation that oversees nine schools in Singapore and a district judge equivalent member of the Valuation Review Board, Ministry of Finance, Singapore, and the Singapore Courts.

INTRODUCTION

Modern Project Management (MPM)— an Artificial Intelligent (AI) Approach

This MPM book is a unique and novel treatment of project management from artificial intelligence (AI) that entails data analytics, deploying neural networks, fuzzy logic, and genetic algorithm(s); and data visualisation, deploying agent-based modelling (ABM) in, for instance, the knowledge-based urban development (KBUD). AI is a technology that replicates activities that normally require human involvement. We have deployed macros in Excel to automate our daily repetitive tasks. We can treat it as the simplest example of AI. Similarly, we did use AI technology in our day-to-day tasks as in modern project management. In fact, AI is more than just simple tasks such as speech and facial recognition or GPS navigation. You can find the quickest travel route to your destination avoiding traffic jams. All such applications are powered by AI. They combine satellite data with current traffic patterns to give you the best route, which is changing and so do work trends. Unlike before, organisations are now deploying project managers as facilitative leaders rather than directive managers. This puts more of the decision-making on the team and empowers them to deliver results faster. AI can help project managers transition to facilitative leaders by taking over routine tasks such as performance reporting.

First and foremost, AI-operated machines can help save organisations money because they don't have to outsource work to contractors. AI will enhance the productivity of employees with higher-quality work and decentralise remote operations. Online workflow platforms are gaining popularities because they give the organisation a larger pool of talent to choose from with flexible working hours. At the same time, artificial intelligence can monitor the process flows to ensure proper protocols are followed, checking resource availability in assigning tasks, providing real-time reporting, and curating self-paced study programs.

Second, AI-powered platform can monitor interactions to facilitate better communications, knowledge transfer, and the likelihood of miscommunication and customer feedback. It is of utmost importance because the relationship between the buyer and the seller has fundamentally changed. The fast and the first is the new formula to win. If you want to win, bring the product to the market first that meets customers' needs. Let AI do the interaction with the customer to figure out what product your customer will want next, while you may focus on developing the product.

Third, while mots projects are unpredictable, AI can help monitor the performance of such projects and allow us to make decisions based on accurate information. AI can help us predict deadlines that might be missed, team member productivity, emerging risks, and quality levels. These predictions will help to calculate the probability of delivering on time, under budget, assignment of the best suitable team member to a specific task, compressing schedules if needed, and response to particular risk. Many decisions have to be taken by leadership and sponsor before the finalisation of the project charter and official approval of the project. Reviewing things like initial versus ongoing investment, make versus buy, risks versus rewards, economic trends and forecasts can take longer time. AI can assist by providing realistic data based on intelligence from similar past projects. Also, it enables senior leaders to select projects that have a higher likelihood of success. Another aspect of initiating projects that AI can help with is making better predictions. Banks are already using AI system for credit scoring to calculate the likelihood you'll pay your loans on time. AI emphasises predictive planning, comprehensive estimation, and automated resource matching. This enables one to streamline our planning and make better AI data-driven decisions rather than relying on our gut instincts. If we take this a step further, AI can add even more value by acting as our digital assistant augmenting everyday planning activities like collecting requirements from stakeholders, tracking assumptions, and archiving business documents and agreements.

Fourth, and if required, AI enables one to find the root causes of deviations from the KPIs and point them out. We can easily identify which KPI needs greater attention with more intelligent data and a real-time view of what's happening on the project. AI conducts 24/7 real-time monitoring and performs predictive analysis and forecasting. Once these insights from past projects are combined with information from current projects, an early warning system can alert with the preventative action. AI introduces structure to the closing process by conducting 24/7 real-time task closing rather than periodic task closing.

The punch line is that we need to anticipate and embrace AI rather than fear it. It is true that some professions and industries are being impacted by AI. For example, the legal profession is currently dealing with digital disruption. AI is imparting lawyer skills by taking over tedious tasks like conducting due diligence on decisions from past cases and applying algorithms to predict the likelihood of winning future cases. Another example is online customer service. Your 80 per cent queries are directly handled by chatbots without any human intervention. The potential impact AI will have on project management and business can be enormous, to enable them to be nimble. Yet AI is purely dependent on precise and reliable data in and data out. Thus, we need the human input of the project manager to rectify or provide the data.

References

CMMI. 2011. *CMMI for Development: Guidelines for Process Integration and Product Improvement*. Old Tappan, NJ, USA: Pearson Education.

PMI. 2013. *A Guide to the Project Management Body of Knowledge (PMBOK® Guide)*, 5th ed. Newtown Square, PA, USA: Project Management Institute (PMI).

Chrissis, M. B., M. Konrad, S. Shrum. 2011. *CMMI for Development: Guidelines for Process Integration and Product Improvement*, 3rd ed. Boston, MA, USA: Addison-Wesley Professional.

PMI. 2013. *A Guide to the Project Management Body of Knowledge (PMBOK® Guide)*, 5th ed. Newtown Square, PA, USA: Project Management Institute (PMI).

Ho. 2020. Forthcoming Book, *Project Management—a Holistic Approach*, Partridge Publishing Co Ltd. Bloomington, IN 47403, USA.

CHAPTER 1

ESTIMATING CONSTRUCTION DEMAND IN SINGAPORE: POTENTIAL OF NEURAL NETWORKS

The aim of chapter 1 is to demonstrate the capability of the state-of-the-art technology of neural network solutions to provide an understanding of the variables of construction demand and to forecast the level of this demand. As the demand for construction is a derived one, this reflects inter-sectoral linkages and associated overall growth with construction activity. The ability to anticipate construction demand in aggregate terms and with respect to various segments offers the opportunity to plan for the expected mix of demand and to affect any necessary strategic restructuring or fine-tuning of the construction industry. As these have been understood in Singapore, efforts are made to predict levels of construction demand. Existing construction demand forecasting models developed for Singapore have conventionally relied on techniques based on statistical analysis to understand the various influencing factors and the relationships amongst them. These models are complex and cumbersome. They are constrained by real-world problems that make it difficult to develop a robust and practical algorithm to forecast construction demand. In particular, when sharp corrections occur in the time series, these models are subjected to repeated model (re)building, testing, and verification to revalidate them in response to the sharp corrections in the time series data. Other problems include the non-stationarity of the data, data scarcity, and structural breaks in the data.

Introduction

In Singapore, the construction share of local gross domestic products (GDP) has steadily climbed from 5.4 per cent in 1989 to 7.1 per cent in 1995. Its output has been growing at 11.9 per cent per annum since 1989. A growing outward trend has been the 'regionalisation' of the local construction industry with the result that there has been an increase in construction firms competing for projects abroad. Contracts won abroad will bring in export earnings to the economy that can offset, in part, the leakages via importation of foreign services and building materials. Besides, with a maturing economy in Singapore, there will be the trend of increasing refurbishment and restoration work in the future. As construction output is a derived demand, it also reflects the importance of inter-sectoral linkages and associative growth. This notion is supported by the high percentage that capital formation in construction contributes to the gross fixed capital formation (GFCF) in Singapore.

The ability to anticipate construction demand enables growth opportunities in terms of emerging markets to be identified. It also has the potential to facilitate the upgrading and strategic restructuring of the industry. It should enhance Singapore's market economy via aiding the fine-tuning of the industry. Finally, the industry's performance over time can be ascertained by establishing the level of production to facilitate comparison with other economic sectors and to enable suitable measures to be adopted to prepare the industry to meet any future changes in the size or nature of demand. The close relationship between Singapore's economy and its construction industry has been established chronologically by Ofori (1988). Therefore, it is advantageous to estimate demand and nurture construction activity to enable it to play its expected role in economic development. Other researchers such as Turin (1973) and Hillebrandt (1984) have also linked the importance of the construction industry to the national economy.

Existing Models

Econometric models used to predict construction demand in Singapore rely on statistical-based approaches to understand the relationships amongst the influencing factors and for forecasting. Most of them have used ordinary and simultaneous least square methods of estimation for model building purposes, with particular contributions from Koh (1987) and work jointly carried out by the Construction Industry Development Board (CIDB) of Singapore and Toh to develop a construction demand model comprising twenty structural equations and twenty identities. In the latter, the equations were estimated individually via ordinary least squares. However, the model is of a proprietary nature and has not been updated over the last three years owing to its complexity. The existing econometric models have been constrained by real-world problems, which make it difficult to develop an algorithm to forecast construction demand. Besides, there is the need to revalidate the variables in the model in response to sharp corrections in the time series data.

This chapter intends to demonstrate the capability of the state-of-the-art technologies, neural network solutions, to explain the variables influencing construction demand. It seeks to develop a demand model using neural network technologies that is explainable. The model should also be robust and adjustable to changes in government regulations, land constraints, and others. To date, structural or explanation-based models in econometrics have been the norm in various studies to establish the relationships amongst economic variables (Bergstrom 1967). These statistical techniques belong to a group of traditional programming techniques. The difficulty here is to develop an algorithm that can simulate real-world complexities. Furthermore, there are inherent problems with time series data—namely, sparse data, non-stationary data, serial correlation, and multi-collinearity. Corresponding corrective techniques have been developed to resolve most of these problems to ensure the robustness of these structural econometric models. However, such econometric approaches are constrained by the need to make assumptions about the time series data and sometimes may limit the parametric analysis to a certain number of possible interactions.

History of Neural Networks

The concept of neural networks first received attention in 1943, when the binary McCulloch-Pitts model showed that even simple types of neural networks comprising two-state threshold elements could, in principle, compute any imaginable computation. This led to research on learning laws by Hebb (1949). Subsequently, the original experimental and modelling work of Hodgkin and Huxley (1952) on the giant squid axon provided the foundation for a series of new models. Rosenblatt (1958) invented the perceptron and showed that 'given linearly separable classes, a Perceptron will, in a finite number of training trials, develop a weight vector that will separate the classes . . . independent of the starting value of the weights'. In 1960, a device called the ADALINE was constructed by Widrow and Hoff, and it was equipped with a new powerful learning law known as the least mean squares or 'delta' rule. However, in 1969, Minsky and Chaptert proved that the single-layer perceptron architecture could not solve Boolean exclusive or XOR problems. The direction shifted to expert systems. Hopfield (1982) rekindled interest in neural networks, and multilayer perceptrons were developed to overcome the XOR constraint. Since then, numerous artificial neural network architectures have been developed. The backpropagation model is amongst the most popular models in use for two reasons:

1. The learning strategy incorporates minimisation of least mean squares (LMS) error across all training patterns whereby this LMS error technique is traditionally accepted.
2. It is a supervised learning, and the network's performance accuracy can be compared with the target training set.

In the field of construction and real estate in Singapore, neural networks have been used in the mass appraisal of private housing using the backpropagation network (BPN) approach; modelling of the overall private housing price index using the general regression neural network (GRNN); and empirical modelling of buildings' indoor air quality using neuro-fuzzy network (NFN).

The Approach

The first stage of the study involved a comprehensive literature review of construction demand models and identification of the indicators that are often used in the prediction of construction demand levels and patterns. Past quarterly data were abstracted from national statistics published by a number of public authorities. The data between first quarter of 1981 and second quarter of 1996 were entered into computer for analysis.

The second stage comprised the training and testing of the neural network model with the selected indicators. To demonstrate the capability of neural networks, the quarterly data between 1981 and 1996 were used for training and developing the model, while 'ex post' forecasts were being made over a historical period between fourth quarter of 1994 and third quarter of 1995. Prediction for the period 1997 to 2000 was also made with assumptions on the future economic conditions of Singapore. The last stage involved the ranking of the various selected indicators in order of their magnitude of influence on the demand factor.

Conceptual Framework

The neural network model seeks to examine the effects of the economy on the construction sector, which, in turn, affects the growth of the economy. Construction demand is deemed to be affected by demand factors, supply factors, and cyclical factors. The conceptual framing of the research problem is shown in figure 1.1.

Fig. 1.1. The conceptual framework

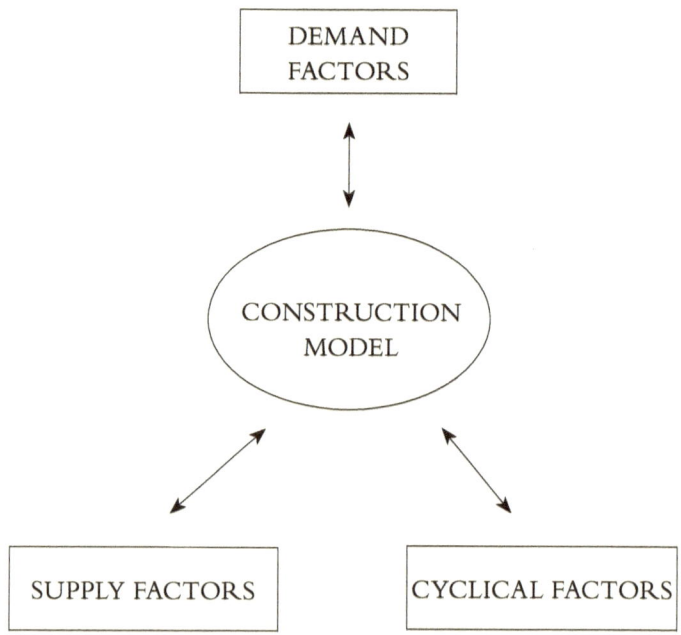

Source: Author (2020).

Examination of the conditions of demand and supply factors relating to the construction industry reveals that its organisation is largely the response to economic factors. This is because an increase in construction efficiency accelerates real estate development, as it will be relatively cheaper to provide a replacement building, and facilitates more intensive development as cheaper capital can be substituted for land (Dipasquale and Wheaton). This leads to the belief that focus should be placed on the demand aspects of the construction industry to enhance economic efficiency. However, the considerations outlined below should be reviewed carefully in the development of the construction demand model.

i. The method of pricing depends on the specifications of the construction project and its components. This reduces opportunities for standardisation and mass production, which, in turn, also depend on the availability of materials, labour, and plant.

ii. The supply of new real estate assets by the construction sector depends on the prices of those assets relative to the cost of replacing or constructing them. In the long run, the asset market should equate market prices with replacement costs that include the cost of land. In the short run, however, the two may diverge significantly because of the lags and delays that are inherent in the construction process. Rent is a key decision factor and demand for space depends on rent and factors such as income levels, firm's production levels, and number of households.

iii. The available data show that at least one-third of the value of the output of the construction industry in Singapore is on repairs and maintenance of the existing stock because buildings are durable.

iv. Construction demand is a derived demand and is subjected to changes in business expectations and fluctuations in the economy.

v. The gross fixed capital formation (GFCF) can be largely accounted for by output from the construction industry during recession period such as in 1985 (Ofori, 1993). The theory of national income approach is meaningful to demonstrate that the changing pattern of private spending (I) and/or government expenditure (G) under different economic conditions can influence construction output and, therefore, its demand level and pattern.

vi. As an investment goods industry, construction is prone to fluctuations in demand resulting from changes in expectations, a rise in the cost of borrowing, and induced changes related to the national income.

vii. In a resource-scarce country such as Singapore, leakages via importation of foreign labour, materials, and plant significantly affect the economy and, hence, construction demand.

viii. Government's budgetary policy plays an important role in construction demand. In Singapore, as private investment decreases during an economic downturn such as the recession in 1985, government spending normally increases to stimulate the economy. On the other hand, a reduction in public spending on capital projects to lessen inflationary overheating reduces overall construction demand.

ix. Construction demand is influenced by the cost of credit and the availability of money, which are administered by the Monetary Authority of Singapore (MAS). Increasing money supply and lowering of credit cost stimulate more investment and, thereby, increase construction demand.

x. Fiscal policy involving changes in tax and subsidies can also affect the rate of real estate development and, thereby, the derived demand for construction.

xi. Land use policies and control mechanisms by the government—for example, the Land Release Programme of the Singapore Urban Redevelopment Authority (URA)—also play a role in moderating the construction demand.

Using the above conceptual framework, the behaviour and response of each variable (factor) admitted into the model must give an in-depth understanding to measure their real impact on the construction demand.

Significant Indicators for Predicting Construction Demand

From the above considerations, these are the significant indicators that influence the level of demand for construction in Singapore and may be used to build the model:

1. prime lending rate
2. money supply (M2)
3. gross domestic product (GDP)
4. gross fixed capital formation (GFCF)
5. consumption expenditure
6. increase in stock
7. manufacturing output
8. building cost
9. 1value of contracts awarded

Adopting these variables, modelling was based on the relationship between the indicators and a suitable demand proxy (i.e., the dependent variable). The value of contracts awarded was chosen as the demand proxy.

Dependent variable

One possible proxy of the dependent variable is the number of development or planning permits issued by the public authorities. However, permits may not translate into actual construction because of changes in demand conditions or escalation of costs beyond thresholds that allow for profitable returns from investment. This leads to the notion that employing space (occupancy) as a demand proxy may not also truly yield the real measure of construction demand unless the market is sufficiently perfect in information dissemination for developers and planners to perceive market performance, expectation, and demand for space (Koh 1987). Another pertinent consideration is that space commenced is concomitantly an indicator of supply although not necessarily specific as space completed. Both Goh (1995) and Tang et al. (1990) chose the value of contracts awarded as the demand proxy. In our model, value of contracts awarded is also admitted as the demand proxy for a simple reason that a dollar change in the value of contracts awarded is a close reflection of the change in the level of construction demand in Singapore.

Independent variables

The remainder of this section is devoted to a discussion of the above-mentioned significant indicators that would be admitted into suitable neural networks as independent variables to examine the influence on construction demand.

Interest rate. Firms invest in plant and equipment in pursuance of the goal to maximise the present value of expectations of future income, and being subjected to the costs of obtaining information, production function constraints, factor supply, and product demand functions. Assuming a perfect capital market, a firm will invest in all projects with internal rate of return exceeding the market rate of interest (Hirshleifer 1958).

Money supply, M2. The model considers M2 as a variable because it is the aggregate amount of money made available to meet societal need. The velocity of money flow can moderate swings in capital investment and spending patterns. The money supply has increased during the last ten years in Singapore, and this strong demand for money can be logically explained by the rapid pace of economic growth. The purpose of incorporating this indicator is to examine the effect of monetary measures adopted by the MAS on the level of construction demand.

Gross domestic product (GDP). GDP is the measure of Singapore's national output in terms of the market value of the output of final goods and services produced within the national boundaries. Throughout the period under review, 1981 to 1996, the national economy experienced growth except in 1985. This economic growth has resulted in a higher level of affluence amongst the people and has been accompanied by more real property developments within the nation.

Gross fixed capital formation (GFCF). Capital investment by the government in the form of infrastructure and buildings has a direct impact on the level of construction demand in Singapore. This has provided many large-scale projects such as the Mass Rapid Transit (MRT) system, the public housing programme, airport and seaport facilities, and expressways/roads.

Consumption expenditure. As more private and public spending is injected into the economy, economic activities become more vibrant. This, in turn, stimulates an increase in the output of the construction industry through new developments such as retail and office space.

Increase in stock. The measurement of the percentage change in stock over previous years is important in two ways. First, the repairs and maintenance account for at least one-third of the value of the output of the construction industry in Singapore and the other is the generation of new capital assets to accelerate economic growth. Second, during the period under review, the increase in stock has also been accompanied by asset appreciation of buildings in Singapore.

Manufacturing output. The performance of the manufacturing industry, especially the electronic and electrical sector, has a strong bearing on the output of the Singapore economy, which, in turn, affects the performance of the construction industry. The perceived boom stage of manufacturing generally fuels asset investment to produce more output, while a slowdown in the performance of this industry may result in shrinkage of asset investment. In essence, construction output is affected by the lagged effect of such a situation.

Building cost. In the context of the study, building cost is a measure of the percentage change in the cost of construction over previous years. The close relationship between building cost and value of contracts awarded can be easily understood by studying the conditions of demand and supply of various factors of production. Locally, materials account for approximately two-thirds of the building cost. Most building materials are imported, as Singapore has no natural resources. Because of a severe shortage of labour faced by the industry, there is also a heavy reliance on relatively inexpensive foreign workers. Plant and equipment are generally imported too.

Neural Networks Theory

A generalised neural network is now presented to explain the theory. Neural networks is a computational technology from the artificial intelligence discipline whose architecture emulates the network of nerve cells in the human brain. In effect, the neural network is a parallel distributed information-processing structure consisting of processing elements (PEs) that contain local memory. The PEs can also carry out localised information processing operations interconnected via unidirectional signal channels called connections (Hecht-Nielsen R 1989).

Figure 2 demonstrates how a neural network architecture—for example, a standard backpropagation neural network—can be developed by using the various indicators as PEs to be investigated upon, and, as in biological systems, the strengths of these connections change in response to the strength of each input and the use of transfer function by the PEs. All nodes (which are indicators) in the input layer are fully connected to each of the hidden nodes in the hidden layer and the process of learning involving all the input nodes and only one of the hidden nodes, H_1. In other words, the learning also involves all the other input nodes with each input node connected to every hidden node. The output value from each node of the hidden layer, in turn, becomes the excitatory input value for a particular node in the output layer.

There are eight indicators—that is, processing elements (PE)—and one bias node in the input layer of the neural network model constructed. All the input values were normalised using the MinMax Table. This is the principle behind this normalisation process:

Normalised value, N

= [Original value less minimum value] / [Maximum value less minimum value]

, where $0 \subseteq N \subseteq 1$. (1.1)

The model learns the underlying latent function through an error gradient-descent method, and the training stops when the root mean square error for output target values generally falls below 5 per cent. Convergence improves when there are more iterations in the training of data. Each hidden node (i.e., H_1 to H_3) receives a set of feed-in signals (or values) from which an output value is generated. Finally, all nodes in the hidden layer are fully connected to the output node.

Fig. 2. A simplified architecture of the backpropagation neural network to model the construction demand

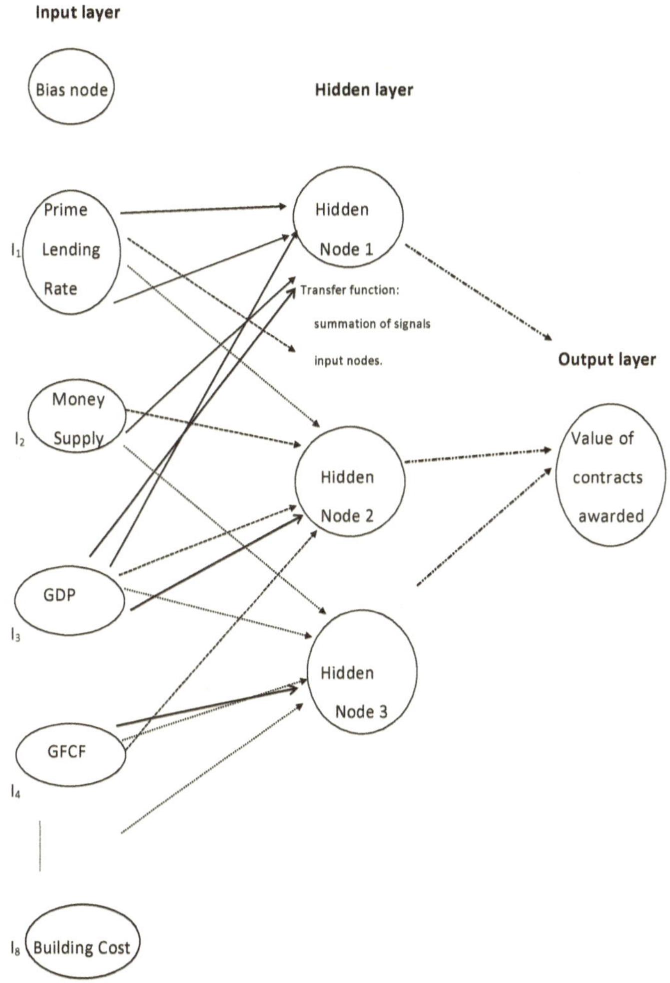

Source: Author (2020).

Causal analysis can be attempted to examine the impact of the various indicators on the value of contracts awarded, the output node. The shares of influence (eq. [2]) for individual input nodes (or indicators) are imputed in the causal analysis. This application of the Garson method (Garson 1991) helps to explain the 'black box' rules in the hidden layer.

Share of Influence Input Node, I_i, asserts on the subject Output Node = S_i%

$$= \frac{\sum_{j=1}[|w_{ij}||o_j| / \sum_{i=1}|w_{ij}|]}{\sum_{i=1}[\sum_{j=1}[|w_{ij}||o_j| / \sum_{i=1}|w_{ij}|]]} \times 100\% \quad (1.2)$$

where,
n_i = number of input nodes;
n_h = number of hidden nodes;
w_{ij} = connection-weight from input node, I_i, to hidden-node, H_j;
o_j = connection-weight from hidden-node, H_j, to subject output node, S_i.

A neural network learns to solve specific problems without the need for problem-specific algorithms. The learning strategy incorporates the minimisation of mean square error across all training patterns, and the network can use supervised training technique with a noise to perturb the network to circumvent the local minima (Hecht-Nielsen R 1989). The desirable result can be dictated, and the network's performance can be compared with the target training set. In the next section, the application of the following three types of neural networks from NeuralWare Professional II (1995) is explained: Fast-learning backpropagation (FBP) neural network, modular neural network (MNN), and the reinforcement neural network (RNN/DRS) using directed random search as the learning rule.

Application of Neural Networks

In the development of feasible neural network solutions, all the eight selected indicators were used to ascertain the effect and to predict the level of construction demand; thereby to preserve consistency in subsequent comparison on the accuracy of neural network solutions.

The fast-learning backpropagation (FBP) neural network was chosen as a basic neural network to compare with two other neural networks, since backpropagation is widely accepted. The modular neural network (MNN) offers a new dimension of learning process through the window of gating network and local experts. However, the global error function is still based on backpropagation of errors. Finally, the reinforcement neural network (RNN) uses DRS to adjust the connection weights rather than backpropagation.

Fast-learning 'backpropagation neural network' is a variation of the traditional backpropagation algorithm presented by Samad (1988). The aim of the learning process is to minimise the global error, E, of the system by modifying the weights. A gradient descent rule is adopted in the learning across the training set. Suppose a vector, i, is presented at the input layer of the network, and the desired output is d. Let o denote the actual output produced by the network with its current set of weights. Then the measure of the error in achieving that desired output is given by:

$$E = 0.5 \cdot \sum_k (D_k - O_k)^2 \qquad (1.3)$$

The MNN consists of a group of networks (referred to as 'local experts') competing to learn the different aspects of the research problem (Jacobs 1991). A gating network controls the competition and learns to assign different regions of the data space to different local expert networks. Both the gating network and the local experts have full connections from the input layer. The gating network has as many output nodes as there are local experts, and the output values of the gating network are normalised to the sum of 1. These normalised output values are used to weight the output vector from the corresponding local expert. The final output vector is the sum of these weighted output vectors. The learning rule is to encourage competition amongst the local experts so that, for a given input vector, the gating network will tend to choose a single local expert rather than a mixture of them. Training of the local experts and the gating network is achieved using backpropagation of error—that is,

$$E = (\mathbf{d}-\mathbf{y})\, dy/dI \tag{1.4}$$

, where
$\mathbf{d}$ = desired output vector (for whole network);
$\mathbf{y}$ = output vector (for whole network).

The RNN with DRS (directed random search) (Matyas 1965) as the learning rule uses a different learning algorithm compared to traditional backpropagation neural network. Random steps are taken in the weight space, and a directed component is added to the random step to provide an impetus to pursue previously successful search directions. The objective of DRS is to choose a set of connection weights that will minimise the network prediction error over all the training cases. In this connection, the prediction error is regarded as the square of the difference between the desired output pattern and the network output pattern for all exemplars in the training set—that is,

$$E = \sum_j (D_j - O_j)^2 \tag{1.5}$$

, where
E = total prediction error;
D_j = desired output of the network for training exemplar j;
O_j = predicted network output for exemplar j.

All the neural networks are set to a certain number of iterations, and training stops when there is convergence at the required root mean square error or when the error across the learning maxim generated by network has become consistently stable. 'Ex post' forecasts are being made over a historical period between fourth quarter of 1994 and third quarter of 1995, and the Run/Test dialog box in the 'Neural Ware' software program will help to establish the actual output. A comparison of the findings presented by the selected neural networks is made to assess the prediction ability of each network solution. The share of influence of various selected indicators is usually established using the Garson's method (Garson 1991). In this regard, the Neural Ware program has the Explain/Now dialog box that shows the change in output caused by the dithering (value is actually the output divided by the input and then multiplied by 100). This mechanism allows us to know which of the indicators has the most effect on the output. A cross-comparison is again made to examine the explanatory ability of the neural network solutions. Finally, a prediction of future level of construction demand between 1997 and 2000 was made.

Results and Findings

This section looks at three aspects of model building. First, the predictive abilities of the neural network solutions are compared. Second, the explanatory strength of indicators on the output PE, value of contracts awarded, is examined. Last, the future level of construction demand between the period 1997 and 2000 is also projected.

a) Historical Forecast: results and their significance

Prediction tests were run on the historical data between fourth quarter of 1994 and third quarter of 1995. The prediction ability of each neural network solution—namely, fast-learning backpropagation (FBP) neural network, modular neural network (MNN), and reinforcement neural network (RNN/DRS) with directed random search as the learning rule are shown in tables 1.1, 1.2, and 1.3, respectively. The STDEV and VAR parameters measure how wide the predicted value is from the actual (historical) value. The results indicate that the neural network solutions are generally robust and acceptable.

Table 1.1. Prediction ability of the backpropagation neural network

YEAR	QUARTER	ACTUAL	PREDICTED	STDEV	VAR
1994	4th	0.9827	1.0144	0.0224	0.0005
1995	1st	1.1139	1.0344	0.0562	0.0031
1995	2nd	1.1910	1.0030	0.1329	0.0176
1995	3rd	0.9693	1.0870	0.0832	0.0069

Source: Author (2020).

Table 1.2. Prediction ability of the modular neural network

YEAR	QUARTER	ACTUAL	PREDICTED	STDEV	VAR
1994	4th	0.9827	0.9352	0.0335	0.0011
1995	1st	1.1139	0.9480	0.1173	0.0137
1995	2nd	1.1910	0.8945	0.2096	0.0439
1995	3rd	0.9693	0.9659	0.0024	5.7800E-6

Source: Author (2020).

Table 1.3. Prediction ability of reinforcement neural network

YEAR	QUARTER	ACTUAL	PREDICTED	STDEV	VAR
1994	4th	0.9827	0.9770	0.004030	1.6245E-5
1995	1st	1.1139	1.1473	0.023617	0.0005
1995	2nd	1.191	1.1938	0.001979	3.9164E-6
1995	3rd	0.9693	0.977	0.005444	2.9637E-5

Source: Author (2020).

Another parameter used in this comparative study is the mean absolute percentage error, MAPE—that is,

$$\Sigma \,|(X_i - F_i)/X_i|\,/n \qquad (1.6)$$

, where
X_i = historical (actual) value;
F_i = predicted value.

The MAPE values of the various neural network solutions are generally below 10 per cent, which implies that the selected indicators may be used as reliable inputs for the modelling of construction demand, and this finding provides further justification for the conclusions drawn by Bon (1989) and Tan (1989) that a close relationship exists between building and economic cycles. In this connection, the prediction ability of reinforcement neural network (RNN)/DRS solution is much more accurate than those offered by fast-learning backpropagation (FBP) neural network solution and modular neural network (MNN) solution. A comparison of their MAPE values shows a 1.15 per cent for RNN(DRS) solution as opposed to 9.57 per cent and 10.04 per cent for FBP and MNN solutions, respectively.

B) Classification of Significant Indicators in Explanatory Strength

$\sum_{i=1} w_{ij} o_j$ is the summation of signal transfers from input to output, and it is shown in column 3 of tables 1.4, 1.5, and 1.6. The tables reflect the relationship between the input signals and the output PE in the respective neural network models. Equation (1.2) is applied to calculate the contribution of individual indicators to explain their share of influence towards the output node, the value of contracts awarded. All three neural network solutions have ranked building cost, manufacturing output, and gross fixed capital formation (GFCF) as influencing factors towards construction demand. The neural network solutions have placed emphasis on these three indicators because they account for a large change in the value of contracts awarded. Besides, they influence the expected mix of construction and pattern of construction demand. The convergence of the ranking of very significant indicators further shows that a few strong variables are of sufficient merit to explain the movement of construction demand, and this is supported by the accumulated shares of influence of these three indicators, being represented by 56.94 per cent (FBP), 60.17 per cent (MNN), and 77.80 per cent (RNN/DRS), respectively.

A unit change in building cost will change the value of contracts awarded. This explains the proportionate relationship between the change in building cost over previous years and the value of contracts awarded. The boom-and-slump effect of the manufacturing industry is directly experienced by the construction industry because a boom offers opportunities for new development and refurbishment projects. Hence, the performance of manufacturing over time can be used to devise suitable measures to prepare the construction industry to meet any future changes in the size or nature of construction demand. The GFCF variable accounts directly for output from the construction industry. Government's capital spending is normally in the form of capital investment to provide a good network of infrastructure and buildings necessary for economic activities and to meet societal needs. Besides, it can be used as an anti-cyclical measure.

Amongst the three neural network solutions, the RNN/DRS offers the strongest explanatory reasoning, shared by the three most significant indicators, for the complexity of the economic behaviour of construction industry.

Table 1.4. Explanatory strength of indicators in the backpropagation neural network model

Indicators	Node	$\Sigma_{j=1i=i=1} [|w_{ij}||o_j|] / \Sigma_{i=1i=i=1} |w_{ij}|]$	Share of influence (%)	Classification by ranking the strength of indicators
Prime Lending rate	2	9.4186	15.35	
Money Supply	3	6.3438	10.34	
Gross Domestic Product	4	5.0684	8.26	
Gross Fixed Capital Formation	5	9.8386	16.03	2

PROJECT MANAGEMENT – AN ARTIFICIAL INTELLIGENT (AI) APPROACH

Consumption Expenditure	6	4.5195	7.37	
Increase in Stock	7	1.0516	1.71	
Manufacturing Output	8	15.343	25.00	1
Building Cost	9	9.7773	15.94	3
Summation of signal transfers		61.3608	100	

Source: Author (2020).

Table 1.5. Explanatory strength of indicators in the modular neural network model

Indicators	Node	$\Sigma_{j=1i=i=1}[|w_{ij}||o_j|] / \Sigma_{i=1i=i=1} |w_{ij}|$	Share of influence (%)	Classification by ranking the strength of indicators
Prime Lending Rate	2	5.7284	10.07	
Money Supply	3	4.3963	7.73	
Gross Domestic Product	4	5.9837	10.52	
Gross Fixed Capital Formation	5	10.5571	18.56	2
Consumption Expenditure	6	5.5695	9.79	
Increase in Stock	7	0.9795	1.72	
Manufacturing Output	8	14.8225	26.05	1
Building Cost	9	8.8564	15.56	3
Summation of signal transfers		56.8934	100	

Source: Author (2020).

Table 1.6. Explanatory strength of indicators in the reinforcement neural network model

Indicators	Node	$\Sigma_{j=1i=i=1}[|w_{ij}||o_j|] / \Sigma_{i=1i=i=1} |w_{ij}|$	Share of influence (%)	Classification by ranking the strength of indicators
Prime Lending Rate	2	10.8203	9.57	

Money Supply	3	8.5475	7.56	
Gross Domestic Product	4	5.6393	4.99	
Gross Fixed Capital Formation	5	11.1028	9.82	3
Consumption Expenditure	6	0.0354	0.03	
Increase in Stock	7	0.0547	0.05	
Manufacturing Output	8	25.573	22.62	2
Building Cost	9	51.2673	45.36	1
Summation of signal transfers		113.0403	**100**	

Source: Author (2020).

c) Future forecast on the level of construction demand

This section predicts the future value of contracts awarded through appropriate assumptions for the eight indicators during 1997 to 2000. Because of the slowdown of the economy during the second half of 1996, the first half of 1997 is assumed to mark a slow recovery. The manufacturing sector is expected to rebound by 1998, and its growth rate is projected at 5 per cent being equivalent to a conservative economic growth rate assumed here. Construction activity is believed to slow down in 1997, but government spending on several major projects will introduce more construction activities from 1998 onwards. Hence, the GFCF is expected to increase by 5 per cent in 1997 to at least 8 per cent in the year 2000. The prime lending rate is expected to remain relatively constant during 1997 to 2000 because the policy is to maintain a healthy economic growth. Based on the past trends, the velocity of money supply (M2) is increasing, and this is expected to grow by 2.5 per cent per quarter. As far as increase in stock is concerned, the projected increase is 5 per cent to reflect a progressively healthy economy. Consumption expenditure may increase moderately by 1 per cent each year. An increase in building cost is justifiable by the strong demand for building materials and the shortage of manpower faced by the construction industry in Singapore. A 5 per cent increase in building cost over previous years is expected.

The foregoing assumptions on the indicators were feed-in in the trained network, and the network is allowed to test the hypothetical data. The results in table 7 and figure 3 show the future forecast of value of contracts awarded ($millions) by the various neural network solutions.

Table 7. Future forecast, the level of construction demand

Quarterly Period 1997 to 2000	FBP network Future Forecast on level of construction output ($million)	MNN Future Forecast on level of construction output ($million)	RNN/DRS Future Forecast on level of construction output ($million)
1st 1997	5295.740	4751.710	4718.126
2nd 1997	5307.249	4758.758	4759.727
3rd 1997	5318.654	4765.727	4801.381
4th 1997	5329.950	4772.610	4843.096
1st 1998	5358.116	4788.241	4921.042
2nd 1998	5369.039	4794.863	4962.770
3rd 1998	5442.241	4852.896	5223.546
4th 1998	5451.911	4858.749	5264.726
1st 1999	5457.942	4857.283	5188.962
2nd 1999	5467.908	4863.088	5230.246
3rd 1999	5477.773	4868.819	5271.400
4th 1999	5487.548	4874.484	5312.410
1st 2000	5492.400	4872.727	5231.024
2nd 2000	5502.031	4878.345	5293.918
3rd 2000	5511.566	4883.893	5313.184
4th 2000	5521.010	4889.376	5354.025

Source: Author (2020).

From the results, the predictions offered by the RNN/DRS appear to converge towards those of the FBP network after the second quarter of 1998. The MNN shows that the construction work volume in terms of value of contracts awarded will be relatively constant over the next four years. The predictions suggest that in 1997 and early 1998, there may be a fall in total workload. From the mid-1998 onwards, there will be some improvements in the construction activities.

Concluding Remarks

Neural networks represent a state-of-the-art approach that intelligently searches for underlying relationships amongst the time series concerned through adapting or changing the connection weights, which represent the array of variables, thereby overcoming the problems associated with sharp corrections, and the paucity and non-stationarity of the data. Unlike the traditional statistical method, which needs a priori parametric knowledge of the form of linear or non-linear function to be tested, neural networks do not need such information beforehand to predict the future possible outcomes. The neural networks were designed to capture the non-linear relationship between the input and output variables automatically. They are useful for solving complex problems that are too difficult to apply constrained-optimisation algorithm. A creative, flexible solution can be 'invented' through neural networks.

Chapter 1 demonstrates the estimating of construction demand via the use of neural network models to predict the output factor, the value of contracts awarded. The results seem to suggest that the RNN/DRS has the best trainability network for the period 1981 to 1996. However, the MNN and FBP networks are still able to offer reasonably good explanatory strength towards the prediction of the level and pattern of construction demand. Neural networks offer a realistic measure of construction demand, which is necessary if effective effort is to be made to maintain, and improve upon, the capacity of the industry. They can also advise on how to moderate the swings in construction outputs through various measures such as monetary and fiscal policies.

Acknowledgement: *The author wishes to gratefully acknowledge the initial work carried out for this original article by Dr Freddie Tan Meng Hor (Nottingham) (Cambridge), vice president of CapitaLand Ltd Singapore overseeing aspects of building technology; and under consultation with honorary professor (University of Hertfordshire, Hatfield, UK), Dr Ho, Kim Hin / David, during their meaningful time before Professor Ho retired from the NUS SDE Departments of Building and Real Estate in May 2019.*

References

Bergstrom, A. R. 1967. *The Construction and Use of Economic Models.*

DiPasquale, D. and W. C. Wheaton. 1995. *Urban Economics and Real Estate Markets.* Prentice Hall, Englewood Cliffs, NJ.

Jacobs, et al. 1991. 'Adaptive mixtures of local experts'. *Neural Computation*, 3, pp.79–87.

Garson, G. D. 1991. 'Interpreting neural-network connection weights'. *AI Expert.* 6, pp. 47–51.

Goh, B. H. 1996. 'Residential construction demand forecasting in Singapore'. *Proc. of Construction Management & Economics*, 14, pp. 25–34.

Hebb, D. O. 1949. *The Organisation of Behavior.* Wiley, New York.

Hecht-Nielsen R. 1989. 'Theory of the Backpropagation neural network'. *Proceedings of the International Joint Conference on Neural Networks*, 1, pp. 593–611. IEEE Press, New York.

Hodgkin, A. L. and A. F. Huxley. 1952. 'A quantitative description of membrane current and its application to conduction and excitation in nerve'. *Journal of Physiology.* 117, pp. 500–544.

Hopfield, J. J. 1982. 'Neural networks and physical systems with emergent collective computational abilities'. *Proceedings of the National Academy of Sciences.* 79, pp. 2554–2558.

Hillebrandt, P. 1984. *Analysis of the British Construction Industry.* Macmillan, London.

Hirshleifer, J. 1958. 'On the optimal investment decision'. *Journal of Political Economy*, 66 No. 4, pp. 329–52.

Koh, A. M. M. 1987. 'An Econometric Model for Forecasting Industrial Space Demand in Singapore'. Unpublished PhD dissertation, University of Georgia, USA.

Matyas, J. 1965. 'Random optimization automation and remote control'. Vol. 26, pp. 246–253.

Minsky, M. and S. Chaptert. 1969. *Perceptrons: An Introduction to Computational Geometry*. MIT Press, Cambridge, MA.

Ofori, G. 1988. 'Construction industry and economic growth in Singapore'. *Construction Management and Economics*, 6, pp. 57–70.

Ofori, G. 1993. *Managing Construction Industry Development: Lessons from Singapore's experience*. Singapore University Press, NUS.

Rosenblatt, F. 1958. 'The Perceptron: A probablistic model for information storage and organisation in the brain'. *Psychological Review*, 65(6), pp. 386–408.

Samad, Tariq. 1988. 'Backpropagation is significantly faster if the expected value of the source unit is used for update'. *International Neural Network Society Conference Abstracts*.

Tang, J. C. S., P. Karasudhi, and P. Tachopiyagoon. 1990. 'Thai construction industry: demand and projection'. *Construction Management & Economics*, 8, pp. 249–57.

Turin, D. A. 1973. *The Construction Industry: Its Economic Significance and Its Role in Development*. University College London.

Widrow, B. and M. E. Hoff. 1960. 'Adaptive switching circuits'. *IRE WESCON Convention Record*, pp. 96–104, New York.

CHAPTER 2

ARTIFICIAL-INTELLIGENCE MODELLING (AIM) OF HONG KONG REAL ESTATE— PRINCIPLES AND CONCEPTS

Chapter 2 introduces the new inter-discipline of artificial intelligence (AI), integrating the disciplines of neuroscience, psychology, and information processing, which has produced five new computational devices that substantially advance the understanding of system dynamics. Neural network (NN), genetic algorithm (GA), fuzzy logic (FL), chaos theory (CT), and expert system (ES) make up such AI devices. They enable an observed system to be modelled under deductive inferencing for ES and FL, and inductive inferencing (or generalised learning in short) for NN, GA, and CT from observed data. In general, AIM allows 'the data to speak for themselves' without making assumptions about the properties of the data but explores a search space of non-linear functions to fit to the observations. Because more of the empirical work has been carried out with neural network in finance and economic research but particularly limited in real estate analysis and forecasting, it will be appropriate to further deepen the knowledge domain of NN and GA. This can be achieved in the specific exercise of forecasting Hong Kong real estate sector by way of its prime residential sector and its inherent markets. The exercise serves a reference purpose.

It is useful to take note that much of the terminology used in NN and GA can trace their roots to the original disciplines. The more commonly known disciplines of econometrics and statistics use different terms to refer to similar concepts. For example, the inputs refer to the independent variables, the outputs to the dependent variables, convergence denotes model fitness in sample, while generalisation denotes out of sample predictions.

Neural Network and Genetic Algorithm

The central processing unit in most computers carry out long sequential instructions at extremely high speeds, in which the computer processes elements of information in a nanosecond (i.e., 10^{-9} sec). Advanced computers can simultaneously carry out a large distribution of instructions in parallel, with in-built error tolerance owing to the presence of a vast number of processing elements. Such a software system is known as a 'parallel distributed information processing' structure or architecture. It offers redundancy for the processing elements and imparts the architecture with learning capability. Therefore, the neural network (NN) is simply a software architecture designed to be a parallel distributed information processing structure of processing elements (PEs). These PEs are interconnected and acquire local memory in their processing operations.

Figure 2.1 briefly explains the working of a simplified NN with the individual PE in the input layer representing the various model inputs. The strength of the PE interconnections will change in response to the strength of each input and the transfer function of the PE. Each of the eight PE inputs is fully connected to each of the hidden nodes in the hidden layer. The output value from each node of the hidden layer, in turn, may then become the critical reached input value for an output layer node. Each hidden node (i.e., H_1 to H_3) receives a set of feed-in values from which an output value is generated. Finally, all nodes in the hidden layer are fully connected to the output layer node. All the eight PE inputs and the corresponding bias are normalised under a typical form—for example, normalised value, N = [Original value less minimum value] / [Maximum value less minimum value] where $0 \subseteq N \subseteq 1$. The underlying latent function is learnt via an error gradient-descent rule applied across the training set's iterations. Suppose a vector I, best visualised as a row of input values giving a snapshot of the output-inputs relationships, is presented at the input layer of the network and the desired output is d. Let o denote the actual output produced by the network with its current set of weights. The knowledge acquired for pattern recognition is captured in the between nodes (i.e., the interconnection) weights, using two functions:

$$x_k = \Sigma_j^n w_{ij} x_k \text{ and } y_o = 1/(1+e^{-x}{}_k).$$

Then the measure of the error in achieving that desired output is given by $E = 0.5. \Sigma_k (D_k - O_k)^2$. It is usual to stop the training when the root mean square error between the output and target values converges to below 5 per cent. Causal analysis can examine the impact of the various inputs on the output layer node. The shares of influence for individual inputs can be imputed via an accumulated error index measurement or the Garson matrix analysis, amongst others.

Fig. 2.1. Fully interconnected network with one layer of hidden units

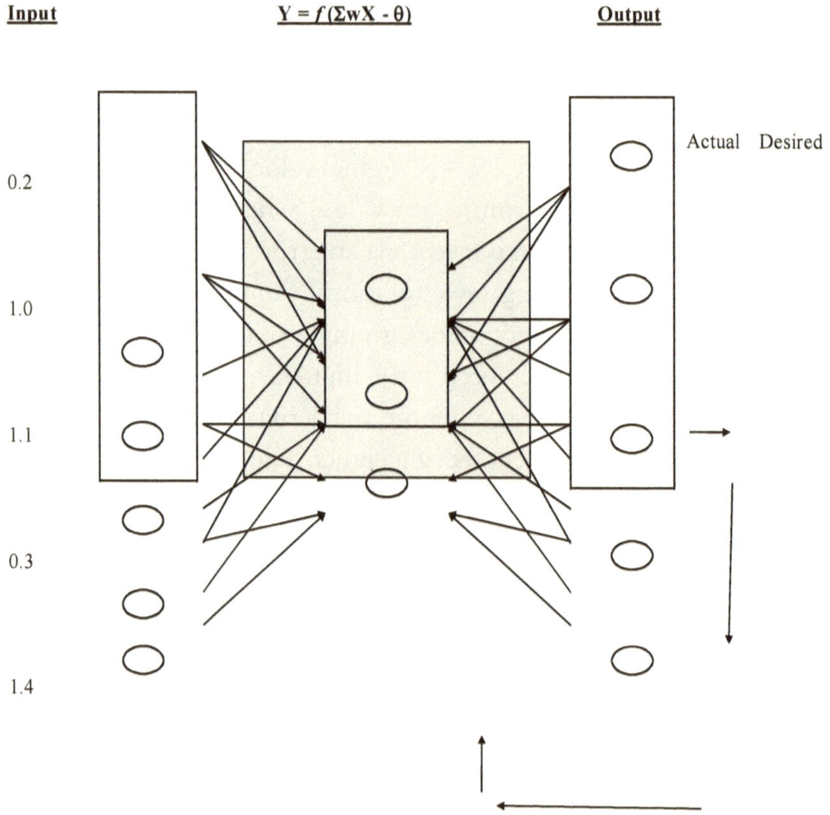

Input $Y = f(\Sigma wX - \theta)$ Output

0.2

1.0

1.1

0.3

1.4

Actual   Desired

Source: Author (2020).

The genetic algorithm (GA) is a powerful search and optimisation procedure based on the principle of natural selection and evolution that has been operating on living species. The GA has a distinct framework consisting of following key components:

- a population of solutions;
- a fitness function to rank each solution in the population;
- ability to combine various members of the population into a new solution (cross-over);
- ability to change a current solution member to a new member (mutation).

GA and neural network can be combined within an integrated neural network architecture in which a genetic search is carried out on the network architecture space of randomly generated networks. Then the NN learning is carried out on the individual networks to evaluate the entire population of networks. This genetic process is mapped out in figure 2.2. Simplistically, the biological genes, which are the units encoding the continuance of life itself, can be envisaged to take the form of a structured network including interconnections. The network then responds to the environment and is selected based on a resulting fitness score. The fittest individual reproduces to yield the genotype in the next generation, and the evolutionary process continues. Cycles of learning are envisaged to be nested within cycles of evolution in populations.

Each learning cycle represents an individual neural network of a particular genetic expression, with a set of input-output pairs from a certain database. The NN learning algorithm then compares the network's actual outputs with the desired outputs and modifies the network's connection weights so that it performs the desired input-output mapping task more accurately. Each evolution cycle processes one population of network designs according to their associated fitness values (computed during the learning cycles) to yield an offspring population of more highly adapted network designs.

Learning takes place under the 'windowing' procedure in which, for example, a window size of three rows (i.e., snapshots) of the values of each input is presented to the network. The learned NNGA model subsequently produces, for example, a ten-year forecast of the individual outputs from, say, June 1999 to June 2010. Windowing also enables the output values to be forecasted in which each output forecast in the next period is imputed from the previous three trained inputs, also themselves forecasted, in a single feed forward pass.

Conceptual Model

The Genetic Algorithm

A genetic algorithm (GA) is a powerful search and optimisation procedure based on the principle of natural selection and evolution that has operated on living species from time immemorial. The GA has a distinct framework consisting of following key components:

- a population of solutions;
- a fitness function to rank each solution in the population;
- ability to combine various members of the population into a new solution (cross-over);
- ability to change a current solution member to a new member (mutation).

Integrated Neural Network and GA

GA and neural network can be combined within an integrated neural network architecture in which a genetic search is carried out on the network architecture space of randomly generated networks, and then the backpropagation learning is carried out on the individual networks to evaluate the entire population of networks. This genetic process is depicted in figure 2.2.

Fig. 2.2. The simplified GA process

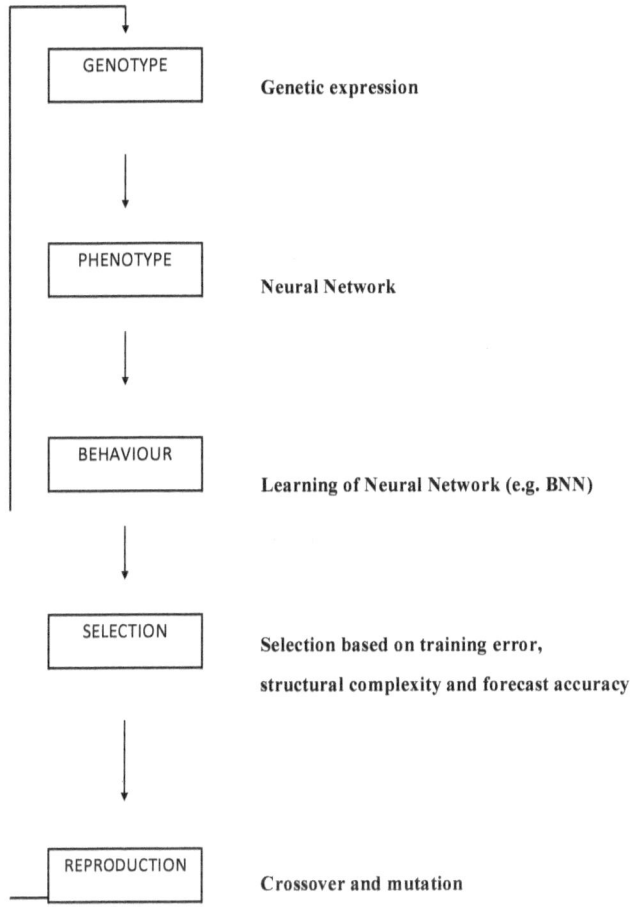

Source: Author (2020).

For ease of understanding and in simplified terminology, the biological genes, which are the units encoding the continuance of life itself, can be envisaged to take the form of a structured network including interconnections. The network then responds to the environment and is selected based on a resulting fitness score. The fittest individual reproduces to yield the genotype in the next generation, and the evolutionary process continues.

Cycles of learning are envisaged to be nested within cycles of evolution in populations. Each learning cycle represents an individual neural network of a particular genetic expression, with a set of input-output pairs from a certain database. The backpropagation learning algorithm then compares the network's actual outputs with the desired outputs and modifies the network's connection weights so that it performs the desired input-output mapping task more accurately. Each evolution cycle processes one population of network designs according to their associated fitness values (computed during the learning cycles) to yield an offspring population of more highly adapted network designs.

The Backpropagation Neural Network (BNN)

The BNN is a regular feedforward network of neurons. The network typically consists of many simple neuron-like processing elements grouped together in layers. Each unit has a state or activity level that is determined by the input received from the other units in the network (see figure 1). Information is processed locally in each unit by computing the dot product between its input vector, o_j, and its weight vector, w_{ji}:

$$x_i = \sum_{j}^{n} o_j w_{ji} - \theta_i \qquad (1.2)$$

, where θ_i is a constant.

Such a weighted sum, x_i, which is called the total input of unit i, is then passed through a sigmoid squashing function to produce the state of unit, i, denoted by o_i. The most common squashing functions are the sigmoidal, the hyperbolic tangent, and the thermodynamic like ones—all of the functional form $Fn = \{f = f(x,k,T,c)|x,k \in R; T, c \in R - \{0\}\}$, which are defined by (2.3):

$$f = \frac{c}{k + 1 + e^{Tx_i}} \qquad (2.3)$$

It is noteworthy that squashing functions vary according to the permissible values of k, c and T. Before training, the weights are initialised with random values. Training the network to produce a desired output vector, o $^{(r)}$, when presented with an input pattern, i$^{(r)}$, involves systematically changing the weights until the network produces the desired output (within a given tolerance). This is repeated over the entire training set. In doing so, each connection in the network computes the derivative, with respect to the connection strength, of a global measure of the error in the performance of the network. The connection strength is then adjusted in the direction that decreases the error. A plausible measure of how poorly the network is performing with its current set of weights is given by E in equation (2.4).

$$E = \tfrac{1}{2} \sum_{j,c}^{n} (y_{j,c} - d_{j,c})^2 \qquad (2.4)$$

, where $y_{j,c}$ is the actual state of the output unit j in input-output case c, and $d_{j,c}$ is its desired state.

Learning is therefore reduced to a minimisation procedure of the error measure given in equation (2.4). This is achieved by repeatedly changing the weights by an amount proportional to the derivative $\partial E/\partial W$, denoted by δ_i:

$$\blacktriangle W_{ij}(t+1) = \lambda \delta_i y_{ij} \qquad (2.5)$$

The learning rate, λ (i.e., the fraction by which the global error is minimised during each pass), is kept constant at least for the duration of a single pass. In the limit, as λ tends to zero and the number of iterations tends to infinity, this learning procedure is guaranteed to find the set of weights that gives the least mean square (LMS) error. The value of $\delta_i = \partial E/\partial W$ is computed by differentiating equations (2.4) and (2.2).

$$\delta_i = (d_{j,c} - y_{j,c}) f^\star(y_i) \tag{2.6}$$

The LMS error procedure has the simple geometric interpretation if we construct a multidimensional 'weight space' that has an axis for each weight and one extra axis called 'height' that corresponds to the error measure. For each combination of weights, the network will have a certain error, which can be represented by the height of a point in weight space. These points form a surface called the 'error surface'. For networks with linear output units and no hidden units, the error surface always forms a bowl whose horizontal cross-sections are ellipses and whose vertical cross-sections are parabolas. Since the bowl has only one minimum (perhaps a complete subspace but nevertheless only one), gradient descent on the error surface is guaranteed to find it.

If the output units have a non-linear but monotonic transfer function, the bowl is deformed but still has only one minimum, so gradient descent still works. However, the hidden units, the error surface, may contain many local minima, so it is possible that steepest descent in weight space will be trapped in poor local minima.

The AIM model building is based on the broad conceptual model of figure 2.3 in which the system dynamics reflect the effects of the economy on the HK office or residential sectors, which, in turn, affects the growth of the economy. The real estate sectoral demand is deemed to be affected by demand factors, supply factors, and economy wide factors.

Fig. 2.3. HK office and residential conceptual model

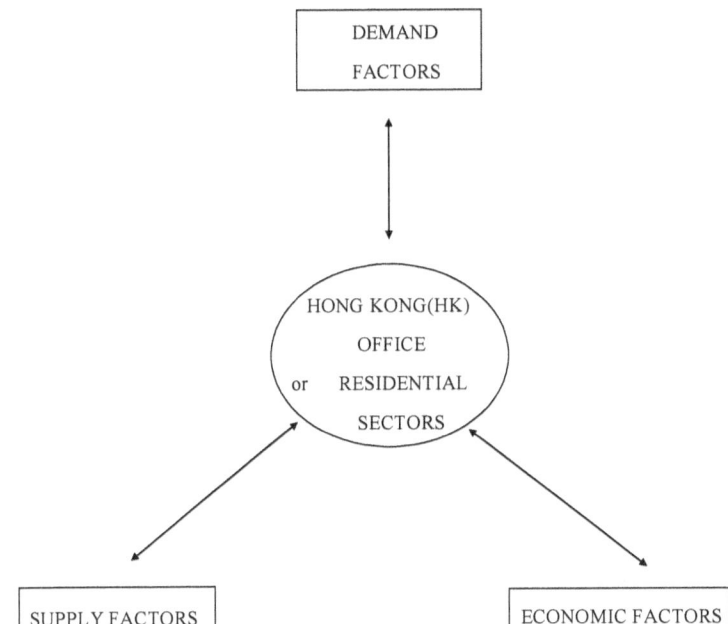

Source: Author (2020).

The conditions of demand and supply factors relating to real estate largely respond to economic factors. This is because expectations of real estate demand will be subject to movements of the business and economic cycles. This leads to greater attention on the aggregate demand issues affecting the real economy and the efficiency issues concerning the real estate sectoral supply and demand.

Concluding Remarks

In general, new private office and residential supply like in Hong Kong (HK) depends on current prices returned by the market relative to the cost of replacing or building them. In the long run, the market should equate market-clearing prices with replacement costs, which include the cost of land. In the short run, however, the two may diverge significantly because of the lags and delays inherent to the building process. Apart from these real estate cyclical factors, land- use policies and control mechanisms—for example, the Land Sales Programme of the Urban Redevelopment Authority (URA) in Singapore—also play a role in stabilising new real estate supply and prices.

Rent is a key decision factor, and the demand for existing/new space depends on rent and factors such as income levels, firm's production levels, and number of households. New supply and demand are also affected by fluctuations in the cost of borrowing and induced changes related to the national income. Private residential demand is influenced by the government's budgetary policy in the building programme of the public housing substitute sector; by the cost of credit and the availability of money administered by the Monetary Authority of Singapore (MAS). Increasing money supply and lowering of credit cost stimulate more investment demand for real estate. Fiscal policy involving changes in tax and subsidies can also affect the rate of real estate development. In this chapter, the NNGA model can be readily adopted to develop the outlooks for the prime HK office sector.

References

Holland, J. H. 1992. *Adaptation in Natural and Artificial Systems*, 2nd edition, MIT Press, Cambridge, MA.

Refenes, A. P. 1995. *Neural Networks in the Capital Markets*, John Wiley & Sons Ltd, Chichester, England.

Tan, P. Y. 1992. 'Automatic Selection of Neural Network Architectures via Genetic Algorithm'. MSc thesis in preparation, National University of Singapore.

Tan, P. Y., G. Lim, K. S. Chua, F. Wong, and S. Neo. 1992. 'A Comparative Study among Neural Networks, Radial Basis Functions and Regression Models'. 2nd International Conference on Automation, Robotics and Computer Vision, September 1992, Singapore.

Tay, P. H. 1994. 'Neuro-Fuzzy Mapping Systems for Real Estate Analysis and Forecasting'. PhD dissertation, Faculty of Architecture and Building, National University of Singapore.

MM High Performance Systems Inc. 2009. 'iThink' software program instruction manual, Mass, USA.

CHAPTER 3

ENERGY RESILIENCY AND SUSTAINABILITY ASSESSMENT—PRINCIPLES AND PRACTICAL CONSIDERATIONS

As the world moves into the reality of peak oil and other types of fossil fuels and alternative energy that begin to fill the growing gap of unceasing energy demand growth, the world cannot procrastinate on the gradual transformation towards sustainability and to the hope for the best. The built environment sector worldwide must find ways to cope with the needs for accelerated and effective implementation of sustainable development and develop and implement measures to build resilience against energy supply shocks and climate change-induced disasters.

The purpose of chapter 2 is to analyse the resiliency and sustainability performance of the innovations, technologies, and system designs developed by the four main centre thrusts. Understanding and modelling of occupant behaviour and preferences, building and energy sector economics, and government policy are critical to this chapter, and, consequently, there will be close collaboration with the human interface and social sciences thrust. The sustainability assessment should apply environmental, economic, and social life cycle-based sustainability metrics to conventional and alternative technologies and strategies. Resiliency assessment will explore how well technology and system level designs will respond to disturbances caused by human and natural systems including energy resource supply disruptions, extreme temperature events, natural disasters, and other catastrophes.

Results provide useful feedback and inform private and public policymakers about future investment and deployment opportunities. Metrics will include life cycle energy and greenhouse gas emissions and life cycle costs of agencies, users, and other stakeholders. In addition, the impact of energy efficiency strategies on social indicators that account for worker comfort and productivity will be evaluated. System resiliency will be assessed for different levels of operability ranging from essential needs (only basic functions met) up to the typical normal levels of performance and comfort. Modelling methods include life cycle assessment (LCA), environmental input-output analysis, geographic information systems (GIS) analysis, agent-based modelling, network analysis, multi-objective analysis, Bayesian statistical analysis, and uncertainty analysis.

The LCA Approach

The LCA approach is particularly relevant. The state-of-art LCA method looks into how changes in demand for a product that is shown to be more environmental friendly can in fact trigger further changes in the 'supply and demand' network in which the product is embedded. This ultimately influences the environmental impact of a product. In this framework, any disturbance may topple the results, and an environmentally friendly product may begin to show more undesirable environmental consequences. This kind of investigation is relevant to the question on resiliency—in this case, the resiliency of low life cycle impact of certain materials and products.

Singapore's economy is extremely trade-dependent, and global supply chains strongly influence the sustainability of the building sector in Singapore. Environmental and economic input/output analysis will be used to study international trade flows of critical materials related to the building sector in Singapore as well as export markets. These model results will help characterise the capabilities and limitations of key technologies and strategies for meeting national energy policy goals. The sustainability assessment will evaluate design and technology innovations and configurations from a systems perspective with respect to life cycle energy, material and water resource flows, and efficiencies. The transformation of the current built environment systems to more resilient and sustainable systems will focus on decentralised buildings with resource harvesting capabilities, highly integrated across building components and functions, and dynamically optimised through novel stressors and controls.

Characteristics and properties of current and proposed future built environment systems are highlighted in table 1. The sustainability assessment will utilise life cycle modelling approaches to evaluate the impact of alternative design and technology solutions on the overall system performance. This requires analysis of energy systems including resource extraction/harvesting, energy conversion, energy storage, and energy utilisation processes. Building materials and systems will also be analysed, accounting for material production, manufacturing and construction, operation, and end-of-life management stages, and accounting for sourcing and transport activities. While Singapore has made significant progress in water management, the chapter team plans to explore wastewater components as an energy source. In addition, dehumidification represents another chapter area that couples water and energy systems.

In addition, this chapter seeks to develop and apply the consequential LCA approach to strengthen conventional methodology. Such approach extends the application of LCA beyond the direct causal effect of a building material and/or component to the consequential impact on the project and industry at large. In this way, the true measure of costs versus benefits of a green innovation may be accurately ascertained. This would be novel to the proposed investigation.

Table 1. Characteristics and properties of current and future built environment systems

Current Built Environment	Future Built Environment
Energy Resources	
Centralised systems for distribution of gas and liquid fuels and electricity generation	Decentralised systems with energy harvesting and storage, utilise diffuse solar radiation and municipal waste and wastewater
Fossil fuels (carbon intensive, high imports, increasing prices)	Renewable (less carbon intensive, less imports)
Material Resources	
Non-renewable and renewable (high imports)	More durable and resilient materials with longer service life (reduce imports)
Passive building material	Intelligent responsive material to environmental changes
Building material for load carrying	Multifunctional materials
Water Resources	
Rainwater collection; water reclamation	On-site closed loop systems, dehumidification sources; utilise wastewater nutrients.
Systems Integration and Resilience	
Building systems not well integrated and not optimised for resiliency.	Smart systems that respond to occupants' needs; systems optimised to maximise resiliency and to minimise resource imports and environmental impacts

Source: Author (2020).

Energy Resilience (ER) and Sustainability models

Energy resiliency is another major model that the proposed project team will develop. Energy resilience (ER) is defined as a building performance quality that is able to provide for a building's strategic flexibility to cope with undersupply or overpricing of energy resources. In such events, a building's operation may need to be partially or significantly curtailed to meet performance needs and cost; hence, supporting a building's management in meeting operational and budgetary limits. By understanding such a model, a building's management can identify critical areas for investment and, at the same time, build in ER during new building design and retrofitting stage. Hence, the ER and sustainability models are significant assessment tools for buildings to cope with the twin challenge of sustainability and resiliency.

Factors influencing the energy resiliency (ER) of a building are shown in figure 1. It shows that a building's ER may be evaluated through a multiple criterion matrix whose impact and corresponding weighting may be determined empirically using the total building performance approach.

Fig. 1. Key factors influencing the energy resilience performance of a building

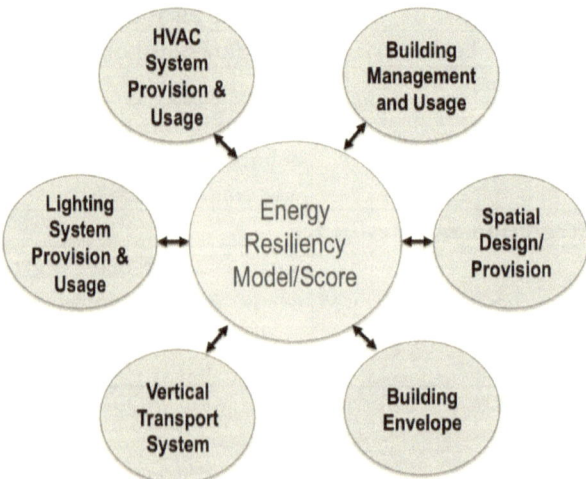

Source: Author (2020).

By understanding the energy performance model and criticality of the various factors influencing the overall ER of a building, a simplified ER model can be developed and studied together with the sustainability model, as shown in figure 2.

Fig. 2. Building resilience model as an integral analysis framework for long-term sustainability of building

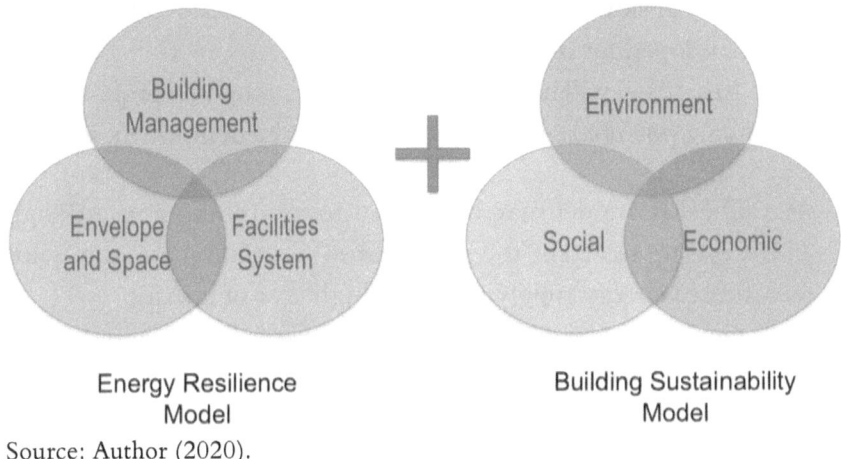

Source: Author (2020).

The ER model of real buildings may be evaluated using a total building performance (TBP) approach. The TBP approach is a framework for examining the performance of building in a holistic and integrated manner. Its approach is user oriented, and, hence, the key performance areas are called performance mandates, as mandated by the users. Using this approach, the overall performance of a building is classified into six performance mandates as follows:

- acoustics performance (aural)
- thermal comfort performance
- indoor air quality performance
- spatial performance
- visual performance
- building integrity performance

A performance matrix can be devised to evaluate and score the performance priority and criticality of a building holistically. The analytical hierarchy process (AHP) will be applied to the empirical results obtained and derive the relationship and indices for the different ER components to form the overall ER model. Combining the various indices of the three key ER components, the energy resilience equation or model may be derived to assess the ER performance of a building using a set of performance indicators. Several models of set of indices may be developed for different building types.

The ER model will be a novel output of the proposed project. It has the following potential contributions to the built environment sector:

- The ER model may be applied to a building at the design stage to ascertain the readiness of a building to cope with future energy supply threat or high cost of energy.
- The ER model may be used to generate solutions and develop management system to cope with future strategic resilience requirement, thus resulting in protective buildings that are better able to meet the challenges of future energy crisis and/or disaster.
- From the analytical hierarchy process, the demand priority of a building may be ascertained, and, hence, investment and protection may be directly the most critical services.

As part of the verification process, case studies will be established using a number of scenarios to test the response of the ER model using the system dynamic modelling (SDM) approach.

Concluding Remarks

In general, the following specific chapter 3 tasks have to be planned to:

1. develop life cycle models and metrics for analysing each technology/innovation. This includes extending the application of the LCA to consequential LCA.
2. compare relative life cycle sustainability performance of each technology/innovation;

3. conduct systems integration of most promising technologies/innovations;
4. develop scenarios for the deployment of technologies/innovations including rates of penetration and develop business as usual scenarios for comparison;
5. develop resiliency perturbation scenarios and model system responses;
6. characterise uncertainties and trade-offs between meeting sustainability and resiliency objectives, and prioritise technology and design options;
7. characterise interconnectedness of system components and develop network models to simulate system responses to internal and external challenges, including consequence analysis as a kind of network modelling. The network, in this case, can be revealed using a technique known as 'technology ecosystem analysis'.
8. develop energy resilience model for a number of key building types using the total building performance (TBP) approach;
9. develop energy resilience score matrix and under empirical studies to ascertain energy resilience index for different building systems and performance mandates;
10. apply the system dynamic modelling method to test the response and behaviour of the energy resilience model using scenario approach;
11. assess the contributions of each technology and innovation to national energy policy goals.

Acknowledgement: *The author wishes to gratefully acknowledge the initial work carried out for chapter 3 by associate professor and fellow Dr Lee, Siew Eang / Anthony (NUS School of Design and Environment, Department of Building), and in consultation with honorary professor (University of Hertfordshire, Hatfield, UK), Dr Ho, Kim Hin / David; during their meaningful brainstorming sessions before Professor Ho retired from the NUS SDE Departments of Real Estate and Building in May 2019.*

References

Randall, Thomas, et al. 1996. *Environmental Design: An Introduction to Architects and Engineers.* Second edition. Personal communication with Dr Freddie Tan M. H., Singapore.

Lang, Jon. 1987. *Creating Architectural Theory: The Role of Behavioral Sciences in Environmental Design.* Personal Communication with Dr Freddie Tan M. H., Singapore.

Tan, F., S. E. Lee, K. H. D. Ho, and W. Schafer. 2003. 'A Fuzzy Logic framework for Intelligent Building (IB) classification for commercial buildings in the tropics'. *Journal of Ambient Energy.* USA.

Priyadarsini, R., W. Xuchao, and L. S. Eang. 2009. 'A study on energy performance of hotel buildings in Singapore'. Personal communication with Associate Professor (Dr) LEE S. E. A., Singapore.

Mahbub, A. S.; H.-W. Kua, and S. E. Lee. 2010. 'A total building performance approach to evaluating building acoustics performance'. Personal communication with Associate Professor (Dr) LEE S. E. A., Singapore.

CHAPTER 4

A FUZZY DISCOUNTED CASH FLOW ANALYSIS FOR THE REAL ESTATE INVESTMENT PROJECT

Chapter 4 brings home the imperative that in a highly complex and volatile world, the investment project analysis tools based on pure probabilistic assumptions are no longer adequate and reliable. Experiences and market knowledge of the project expert may effectively reduce the margin of variations of the market forecasts. But the translations of these project expert knowledge that are imprecise and vague in the representations are the obstacle to the application of the expert knowledge. The fuzzy discounted cash flow (DCF) model provides a natural and intuitive way of dealing with the problems of fuzziness and cognitive uncertainty. Based on a set of fuzzy inputs, the fuzzy net present value (NPV) for the case of an office-cum-retail development is calculated to provide an approximated evaluation of the investment interest. The result of the fuzzy DCF analysis, after the centroid defuzzification process, shows a positive cash flow of S$8,532,785. It was an increase of 53.38 per cent compared with the NPV estimated by the classical DCF model. The differences reflect partly the trade-off involved in generalising the classical model and the assumption of the uncertainty.

Traditional non-discounting techniques for investment project analysis such as the payback period and the accounting rate of return have been criticised for neglecting the time value of money. It is widely observed that during the period of high inflation, the time value of money is critical in the investment decision process. Real returns of many profitable projects are reduced and payback periods of investments are prolonged because of the erosion of the real value of money. With much progress in the field of financial economics, the time value of money has been explicitly reflected as a key principle in the discounted cash flow (DCF) technique for investment. Such a technique is increasingly used in financial management, economic analysis, and property valuation to provide more precise cash flow projection and evaluation for investment projects.

In the DCF technique, the reliability and credibility of the results are strictly dependent on the projection and prediction of the essential input variables. These variables are deterministic, and their variations are invariably probabilistic in nature. There are two approaches at which these inputs can be rigorously determined. The first approach involves the use of the standard statistical tools such as the multiple regression analysis and the Box-Jenkins time series models. Such an approach is nonetheless not unfettered by various statistical errors. By adhering to the probabilistic assumptions of the models, the meaning and value of the input estimates are also limited and bounded by the likelihood of historical occurrences. In a complex world, randomness alone is insufficient and unrealistic to capture the dynamics and changes in real-world events.

The second approach in favour of the formal quantitative models are based on the *ex-ante* expert judgement of the near term event. Disregarding judgemental biases, experts with sufficient information and reasonable knowledge of the market are able to approximate the performance of a particular real asset within an acceptable confidence interval. The expert knowledge may intuitively be more reliable than the ex post estimates of the formal models (Makridakis and

Wheelwright 1979). However, constrained by the complexity and uncertainty of information in reality (Zadeh 1977), the expression of the expert knowledge is vague and imprecise (von Winterfeldt and Edward 1986), and it is also inconsistent with the corresponding expression under mathematical modelling (Fischhoff 1989). In most instances, project experts express their judgement, and investors perceive their risk and return preferences in cognitively vague and ambiguous forms. For instance, a judgement of a 'weak' office property market by an expert may be reflected by a per-square-foot rental of S$6 to S$8. An 'average' return in the expectation of a risk-averse investor may imply an annual return of not less than 8 per cent with a standard deviation of 0.5.

The Fuzzy Dictum

This source of cognitive uncertainty, which is associated with the subjectivity of human thinking and reasoning, is collectively known as 'fuzziness'. It is not merely concerned with the membership of a point in a set, but it relates to the gradual progression from a membership to a non-membership function (Gupta 1977). In other words, there is a 'possibility' dimension added to the information, which is conceptually different from the probabilistic angle that emphasises the crispness and precision of representation. For example, an expert's prediction of a unit office space rental of S$6 to S$8 per square foot can be translated by a simple average into an exact S$7 per-square-foot rental. It discretely eliminates other possible values on either sides of the boundary like SS$6.5 or S$7.5, etc. Failure to capture this form of 'fuzziness' may lead to miscalculations and misjudgement in the analysis.

As a new and theoretical construct, fuzzy set theory permits the trade-off between precision and vagueness of the available information to provide an intuitively sounder result (Klir and Folger 1992). In the context of the DCF technique, the generalisation of cash flow projections will relax the strict translation of expert knowledge, which is usually defined in crisp terms. This offers a more natural way of representing and incorporating the experts' estimates of the variables in the cash flow. Buckley (1987) sacrifices the 'precision' of the input estimates in the traditional DCF analysis with the adoption of inexact 'fuzzy' numbers to define interest rate, the cash amounts, and a positive discrete fuzzy set to represent the duration of an investment. He generalises the compound interest concept through the use of the fuzzified variables without compromising the reliability of the DCF outcome and, hence, the quality of the cash flow streams.

Chapter 2 seeks to analyse a real estate development project adopting the fuzzy DCF models proposed by Buckley (1987). It then compares the results with those estimated by the traditional methods. The results of the fuzzy NPV by themselves make no sense to the investor, and we propose to 'defuzzify' the fuzzy solutions using the 'centroid defuzzification' methodology to arrive at the optimal non-fuzzy NPV. Chapter 2 is organised into five sections. The first section reiterates the importance of the concepts of 'fuzziness' and the limitations of the traditional DCF technique. The latter does not take into account the imprecision and vagueness inherent in the predictions and assumptions of the essential variables. The next (second) section conceptualises the fuzzy compound interest formula, while the third section defines the decision criteria of the fuzzy DCF model, proposed by Buckley (1987). An illustrative comparison between the fuzzy and traditional DCF models for a prime office development project is covered in the fourth and fifth sections. The last (sixth) section concludes the analysis.

Concepts of Fuzzy Compound Interest

In the fuzzy DCF model, three fuzzy compound interest concepts are introduced: the fuzzy future value, the fuzzy present value, and the fuzzy present value of annuity factors. The concepts of the fuzzy compound interest involve four essential variables: fuzzy present value ($\overline{A}$), fuzzy future value ($\overline{S}$), fuzzy interest rate per period ($\overline{r}$

), and the number of compounding periods, which can be a crisp number (n) or a discrete positive fuzzy number ($\bar{n}$), where $\mu(ni|\bar{n}) = \lambda$, $0 \leq \lambda \leq 1$ for $1 \leq i \leq k$ such that k is the collection of the fuzzy number ni. For $x \neq ni$, $\mu(x|\bar{n}) = 0$. The value of λ measures the possibility of the compounding period being n_i given $\bar{n}$ is a fuzzy number. In formulating the fuzzy compound interest factors, a LR-type (left-right) fuzzy number $(m_1/m_2, m_3/m_4)$, as adopted by Buckley (1987), is used. Its membership function of figure 4.1 is represented by a unique increasing function f_1 and a decreasing function f_2 is defined by equation (4.1).

$$\mu(x|\overline{M}) = (m_1, f_1(y|\overline{M}/m_2, m_3/f_2(y|\overline{M}, m_4) \quad (4.1)$$

Fig. 4.1. Graph of μ(x|$\overline{M}$): the membership function for fuzzy number M

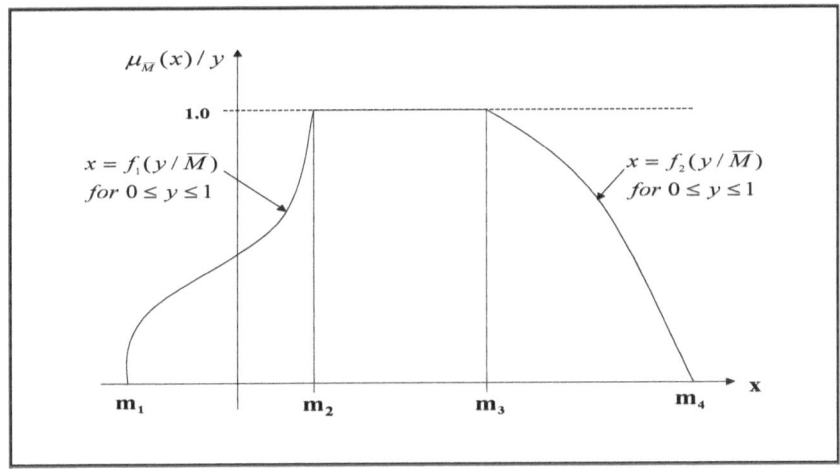

Source: Author (2020).

The Fuzzy Future Value

The fuzzy future value is a fuzzy lump sum ($\bar{S}_n$) that a fuzzy amount of $\bar{A}$ invested today at a fuzzy interest rate of $\bar{r}$, accumulates to the n period in the future. Given that $\bar{A}$ and $\bar{r}$ are fuzzy positive numbers, then

$$\bar{S}_n = \bar{A} \otimes (1 \oplus \bar{r})^n \qquad (4.2)$$

, where $\otimes$ and $\oplus$ are the extended fuzzy multiplication and addition.[1] The membership function for $\bar{S}_n$ is

$$\mu(x|\bar{S}_n) = (s_{n1}, f_{n1}(y|\bar{S}_n)/s_{n2}, s_{n3}/f_{n2}(y|\bar{S}_n), s_{n4}) \qquad (4.3)$$

If the number of compounding periods $\bar{n}$ is also a fuzzy number, then the membership function of the fuzzy future value is defined by

$$\mu(x|\bar{S}) = \max_{1 \leq i \leq k} \left[\min(\mu(x|\bar{S}_{ni}), \lambda_i) \right] \qquad (4.4)$$

, where λ_i as defined earlier, is the membership function of the compounding periods n_i. Equation (4.4) modifies the membership function of $\bar{S}_n$ as in equation (4.2) from the distribution at a height of λ_i (the membership function of $\bar{n}$). For an illustration, consider an asset having a current market value of $\bar{A}$ and a compounding growth rate of $\bar{r}$, the future worth of the asset in two year time is $\bar{S}_2$, which can be determined as a fuzzy number—that is,

Market Value ($\bar{A}$) = ($239,450,000/$239,500,000,S$240,000,000/$240,100,000)

Capitalisation Rate ($\bar{r}$) = (2.5%/3%, 4%/4.2%)

Market Value in Year 2 ($\bar{S}_2$)

$\bar{S}_2$ = ($239,450,000/$239,500,000,S$240,000,000/$240,100,000) $\otimes$ [1 $\oplus$ (2.5%/3%, 4%/4.2%)]^2

---

[1] Please refer to Dubois and Parade (1979) for the technical details of the extended fuzzy arithmetic operations.

$\overline{S}_2$ = ($253,046,929/$253,099,768,S$260,583,360/$260,691,936)

If $\overline{n}$ is a fuzzy number with membership function of λ = 0.85, then the fuzzy market value in year two is determined at the cut-off level of 0.85 as shown in figure 4.2. Assuming that the increasing $f_1(y|\overline{S}_n)$ and the decreasing $f_2(y|\overline{S}_n)$ parts of $\mu 2(x|\overline{S}_n, n)$ are linear, x_1 and x_2 can be determined in the following manner,

$$x_1 = f_1(y|\overline{S}) = (\overline{S}_2 - \overline{S}_1)y + \overline{S}_1 \qquad (4.5a)$$
$$x_2 = f_2(y|\overline{S}) = (\overline{S}_3 - \overline{S}_4)y + \overline{S}_4 \qquad (4.5b)$$

Fig. 4. 2. The fuzzy market value in year two

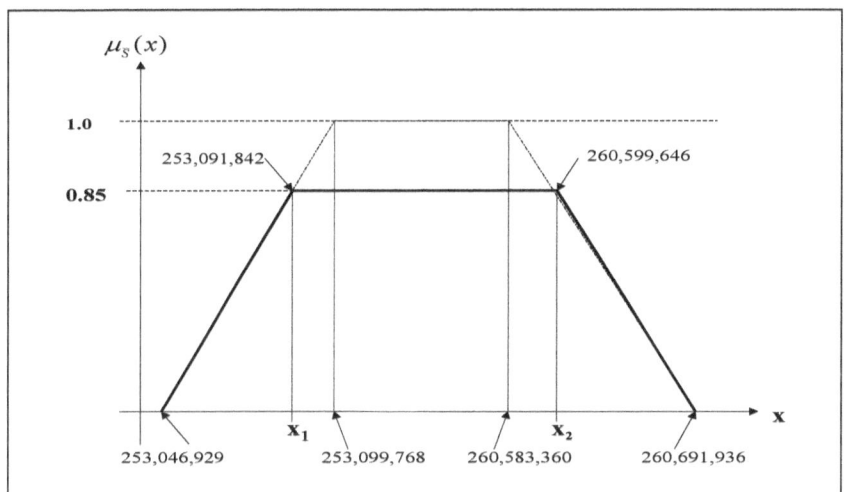

Source: Author (2020).

At the cut-off point where the value of y is 0.85, then x_1 and x_2 are calculated as S$253,091,842 and S$260,599,646, respectively.

The Fuzzy Present Value

A fuzzy present value $\overline{A}$ is defined as the current worth of a fuzzy lump sum $\overline{S}$ that will be received in *n* periods in the future. Given that the fuzzy interest rate per period $\overline{r}$ is a fuzzy positive number and $\bar{S}$ is either a positive or a negative fuzzy value, two definitions of the fuzzy present value ($\bar{A}$) are provided:

Definition 1:

$PV_1(\bar{S}, n) = \bar{A}$ if and only if (iff) $\bar{A}$ is a fuzzy number and $\bar{A} \otimes (1 \oplus \bar{r})^n = \bar{S}$, such that $\bar{S}$ is negative. Therefore,

$$PV_1(\bar{S}, n) \otimes (1 \oplus \bar{r})^n = \bar{S} \qquad (4.6)$$

The membership function $\mu_1(x|\bar{S}, n)$ for $PV_1(\bar{S}, n)$ with negative $\bar{S}$ is determined by

$$f_i(y|\bar{A}) = f_i(y|\bar{S}) * [1 + f_i(y|\bar{r})]^{-n} \qquad (4.7)$$

for i = 1,2 and $a_1 = f_1(0|\bar{A})$, $a_2 = f_1(1|\bar{A})$, $a_3 = f_2(1|\bar{A})$, $a_4 = f_2(0|\bar{A})$. Therefore, $PV_1(\bar{S}, n) = \bar{A}$, iff $f_1(y|\bar{A})$ is increasing and $f_2(y|\bar{A})$ is decreasing and $a_2 \leq a_3$.

Definition 2:

$PV_2(\bar{S}, n) = \bar{A}$ if and only if $\bar{A}$ is a fuzzy number and $\bar{A} = \bar{S} \otimes (1 \oplus \bar{r})^n$, such that $\bar{S}$ is positive. Therefore,

$$PV_2(\bar{S}, n) \otimes (1 \oplus \bar{r})^n \cong \bar{S} \qquad (4.8)$$

The membership function of $\mu_2(x|\bar{S}, n)$ for $PV_2(\bar{S}, n)$ with positive $\bar{S}$ is determined by

$$f_i(y|\bar{A}) = f_i(y|\bar{S}) * [(1 + f_{3-i}(y|\bar{r})]^{-n} \qquad (4.9)$$

for i = 1,2 and $a_1 = f_1(0|\bar{A})$, $a_2 = f_1(1|\bar{A})$, $a_3 = f_2(1|\bar{A})$, $a_4 = f_2(0|\bar{A})$. Then $PV_2(\bar{S}, n) = \bar{A}$, a fuzzy number, iff $f_1(y|\bar{A})$ is increasing and $f_2(y|\bar{A})$ is decreasing and $a_2 \leq a_3$.

If $\bar{n}$ is a fuzzy number, then the membership function for both the present value $PV_1(\bar{S}, n)$ and/or $PV_2(\bar{S}, n)$ is defined by

$$\mu_1(x|\bar{S}) = \max_{1 \le i \le k}\left[\min(\mu(x|\bar{S},\bar{n}), \lambda_i)\right] \qquad (4.10)$$

Based on equation (4.8), the following illustrates the computation of the present value of a fuzzy lump sum of $\bar{S}_3$ in year three in the future discounted at a fuzzy interest rate of:

Lump sum value in year 3 ($\bar{S}_3$)

$\bar{S}_3$ = ($65,095,958/$68,214,193,S$85,527,659/$88,818,865)

Expected rate of return ($\bar{r}$) = (8%/9%, 9%/12%)

$PV_2(\bar{S} | n_3) \cong$ ($65,095,958/$68,214,193, 85,527,659/$88,818,865) $\otimes$

$[1 \oplus (8\%/9\%, 9\%/12\%)]^3$

$PV_2(\bar{S} | n_3) \cong$ ($46,334,017/$48,553,515,S$67,894,613/$70,507,079)

Assuming that the membership function of n_3 is 1.0, then $\min(\mu(x|\bar{S}, n_3), \lambda_3)$ is equivalent to $\mu(x|\bar{S}, n_3)$. The possibility distribution for the fuzzy present value is shown in figure 4.3.

Fig. 4 3. Fuzzy present value for year three terminal cash flow

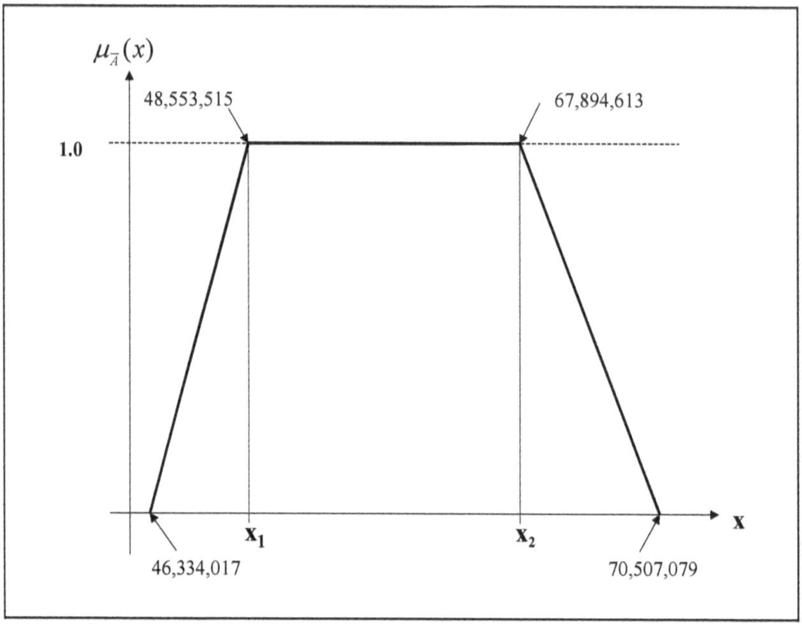

[Figure: Trapezoidal fuzzy membership function $\mu_{\bar{A}}(x)$ with values 46,334,017; 48,553,515 (x_1); 67,894,613 (x_2); 70,507,079]

Source: Author (2020).

Fuzzy Present Value of Annuity

Assume that fuzzy payments are made at the end of each period for n periods at a fuzzy interest rate $\bar{r}$. $\bar{A}_n$ represents the present worth of the accumulation of a stream of fuzzy payments $\bar{P}$. If both $\bar{P}$ and $\bar{r}$ are positive fuzzy numbers, the present value of the fuzzy cash flow is given as

$$\bar{A}_n = \bar{P} \otimes \gamma(n,\bar{r}) \tag{4.11}$$

$\bar{P}$ is known as fuzzy regular annuity, and $\lambda(n, \bar{r})$ is the fuzzy present value factor defined as

$$\gamma(n,\bar{r}) = [1 \ominus (1 \oplus \bar{r})^{-n}] \otimes \bar{r}^{-1} \tag{4.12}$$

, where y is the extended fuzzy subtraction operator. The membership function $\mu(x|\bar{A}_n)$ of $\bar{A}_n$ is determined by

$$f_{ni}(y|\bar{A}_n) = f_i(y|\bar{P}) * \gamma(n, f_{3-i}(y|\bar{r})) \qquad (4.13)$$

for i = 1,2 and $a_{n1} = f_{n1}(0|\bar{A}_n)$, $a_{n2} = f_{n1}(1|\bar{A}_n)$, $a_{n3} = f_{n2}(1|\bar{A}_n)$, and $a_{n4} = f_{n2}(0|\bar{A}_n)$.

If the number of payment periods $\bar{n}$ is a fuzzy number, the membership function of $\bar{A}_n$ is defined as

$$\mu(x|\bar{A}) = \max_{1 \le i \le k}\left[\min(\mu(x|\bar{A}_n), \lambda_i)\right] \qquad (4.14)$$

To illustrate the concept of fuzzy present value of annuity, the imputation of the fuzzy annual debt service for a mortgage loan of 80 per cent of an asset market value of $\bar{A}$ is provided below:

Term of loan (n) = 20 years
Loan to value ratio = 80%
Interest rate (r) = 6.5%
Market value of an asset,

$(\bar{A})$ = ($,239,450,000/$239,500,000,S$240,000,000/$240,100,000)

Loan principal = $0.8 \otimes \bar{A}$

= ($191,560,000/$191,600,000,S$192,000,000/$192,080,000)

Annual debt service $(\bar{P}) = (0.8 \otimes \bar{A}) \otimes \lambda(n,r)$
and with $\bar{P}$ = ($17,385,295/$17,388,925,S$17,425,228/$17,432,488).

Fuzzy Discounted Cash Flow Models

Fuzzy DCF models are essentially concerned with discounting a stream of expected future cash flows represented by positive or negative fuzzy numbers, over an expected holding period n, at a fuzzy rate of return. There are two types of fuzzy DCF models: the fuzzy net present value (NPV) model and the fuzzy internal rate of return (IRR).[2]

In the case of fuzzy NPV model, consider a fuzzy net cash flow stream, $\overline{\Lambda} = \overline{A}_0, ..., \overline{A}_n$ and a fuzzy interest rate, $\overline{r}_0$, the membership function $\mu(x|\overline{A}_i)$ of the fuzzy number $\overline{A}_i$ is defined by

$$\mu(x|\overline{A}_i) = (a_{i1}, f_{i1}(y|\overline{A})/a_{i2}, a_{i3}/f_{i2}(y|\overline{A}_i), a_{i4}) \qquad (4.15)$$

for i = 0,1,....., n. $\overline{A}_0$ is a negative fuzzy number and the other $\overline{A}_i$ are either positive of negative fuzzy numbers. The rate $\overline{r}_0$ is a positive fuzzy number. The fuzzy net present value of $\overline{\Lambda}$ is given as

$$NPV(\overline{\Lambda}, n) = \overline{A}_0 \oplus \sum_{i=1}^{n} PV_{k(i)}(\overline{A}_i, i) \qquad (4.16)$$

, where Σ is the fuzzy summation. K(i) = 1 when $\overline{A}_i$ is negative and K(i) = 2 for a positive $\overline{A}_i$.

The membership function $\mu(x|\overline{\Lambda},n)$ of the NPV($\overline{\Lambda}$,n) is defined by

$$\mu(x|\overline{A},n) = (\alpha_{n1}, f_{n1}(y|\overline{A})/\alpha_{n2}, \alpha_{n3}/f_{n2}(y|\overline{A}), \alpha_{n4}) \qquad (4.17)$$

, where

$$f_{ni}(y|\overline{A}) = \sum_{j=0}^{n} f_{ji}(y|\overline{A}_j) * \left[1 + f_{k0}(y|\overline{r}_0)\right]^{-j} \qquad (4.18)$$

---

[2] The fuzzy IRR model has been shown to be an inappropriate extension of cash flow analysis under fuzzy representation by Buckley (1987).

PROJECT MANAGEMENT – AN ARTIFICIAL INTELLIGENT (AI) APPROACH

for i = 1,2, where k(j) = 1 for a negative $\overline{A}_j$ and K(j) = 3 - i for a positive $\overline{A}_j$, so that $\alpha_{n1} = f_{n1}(0|\overline{\Lambda})$, $\alpha_{n2} = f_{n1}(1|\overline{\Lambda})$, $\alpha_{n3} = f_{n2}(1|\overline{\Lambda})$, $\alpha_{n4} = f_{n2}(0|\overline{\Lambda})$.

If the expected holding period is a discrete positive fuzzy number $\overline{n}$, the membership function of the fuzzy net present value NPV($\overline{\Lambda}$, $\overline{n}$) is generalised as follows:

$$\mu(x|\overline{\Lambda}) = \max_{1 \leq i \leq k} \left[\min(\mu(x|\overline{\Lambda}, n_i), \lambda_i) \right] \quad (4.19)$$

The decision-making rule under fuzzy NPV requires that the NPV exceed $\overline{0}$ for a project to be accepted, where $\overline{0}$ is some appropriate representation of fuzzy zero. Therefore,

if NPV is positive (i.e., $\alpha_1 \geq 0$), then the project is accepted; and if NPV is negative (i.e., $\alpha_4 \leq 0$), then reject the project.

Case of an Office-Cum-Retail Development

Using an office-cum-retail development as a case study, the feasibility of the investment is first analysed under the classical DCF model. The cash flow of selected variables is then generalised and the NPV based on the projected fuzzy cash flows is computed. The differences in the results of the two models are compared to examine the effects of cognitive uncertainty.

Case Profile and Assumptions for the Input Variables

The subject direct real estate asset is a ten-storey office-cum-retail development located in the Central Business District of Singapore. The subject asset comprises eight floors of offices with a total net lettable area of 26,092.3 square meters. The remaining two floors are occupied by a restaurant and shops with net lettable areas of 1,342.2 sqm and 1760.6 sqm respectively. The subject asset is built in 1973 on a land area of 6,147.9 sqm and with a leasehold interest of ninety-nine years. Based on-site surveys and market analyses, the following information are acquired:

i. The market value of the subject direct real estate asset is estimated at S$240,000,000. The acquisition cost includes legal fees, professional fees, and stamp duty is 4 per cent. The capital appreciation rate is estimated at 3.4 per cent. The cost of sale is 4 per cent.
ii. A long-term loan of twenty years is granted by a bank at an annual interest rate of 6.5 per cent, subject to the maximum loan to value ratio of 80 per cent (i.e., the loan principal = S$192,000,000). The annual debt service is imputed as S$17,425,228.
iii. The gross monthly rental is S$53.80 psm (S$5 psm) for offices and S$ 207.60 psm (S$10 psf) for retail space and a restaurant. A 5 per cent vacancy rate is observed. The annual rental growth rate is assumed to be 3.4 per cent, and the leases are subject to a three-year rent revision term.
iv. The 4stores basement car park is expected to generate a net revenue of S$600,000 p.a.
v. The operating expenses are 15 per cent of the gross revenue. The direct real estate tax rate is 16 per cent of the effective gross rental, while the corporate tax is 30 per cent of the before-tax cash flow.
vi. The investor holds the direct real estate asset for a period of five years and for an expected return of 9 per cent per annum.

Assumptions for the Fuzzy Input Variables

For the fuzzy DCF analysis, the after-tax cash flows (AFCT) are projected on the basis of the following selected fuzzified input variables—that is, variables that are expressed vaguely and imprecisely by fuzzy numbers.

i. The market value is around S$239,500,000 to S$240,000,000, and the rate of capital appreciation is not more than 4 per cent and not less than 3 per cent. The cost of acquisition and cost of sale are about 4 per cent each.

ii. The gross monthly rental for offices is about S$54 psm, and for retail space and a restaurant, it ranges approximately between S$200 psm and S$210 psm. The vacancy rate remains at around 5 per cent but is not be more than 6 per cent. The annual rental growth rate is approximately 3.4 per cent.

iii. The car park revenue is more or less S$600,000 per annum.

iv. The operating expenses are more than 10 per cent.

v. The holding period of the investment is not more than six years and with the possibility of each period being indicated by λ_i in table 4.1.

Table 1. Possibility distribution of the number of holding period in year

n	1	2	3	4	5	6
λ_i	0.8	0.85	1	1	0.9	0.7

Source: Author (2020).

vi. The expected rate of return *is not less than 8 per cent.*

Other variables like the direct real estate tax rate and the loan terms are assumed to be deterministic and represented earlier (first section) by the crisp numbers. The foregoing fuzzy variables are formally represented by the LR-type fuzzy numbers with linear continuous monotone increasing and decreasing functions, and they are summarised in table 4.2.

Table 2. Fuzzy variables and their LR fuzzy representations

Input Variables	The LR fuzzy representation
Market value ($ million)	($239.45,S$239.50,S$240.00,S$240.10)
Capital appreciation rate (% p.a.)	(2.50%, 3.00%, 4.00%, 4.20%)

Gross monthly rental for offices ($ p.mth.)	($50.00, S$54,00, S$54.00, S$59.00)
Gross monthly rental for retail and restaurant ($ p.mth.)	($195.00, S$200.00, S$210.00, S$220.00)
Vacancy rate (%)	(4.00%, 5.00%, 6.00%, 6.50%)
Rental growth rate (% p.a.)	(3.00%, 3.40%, 3.40%, 4.00%)
Net car park revenue ($'000)	($560.00, S$600.00, S$600.00, S$650.00)
Operating expenses (% of gross revenue)	(10.00%, 11.00%, 11.00%, 15.00%)
Expected rate of return (%)	(8.00%, 9.00%, 9.00%, 12.00%)
Costs of acquisition and sale (% agreed prices)	(3.80%, 4.00%, 4.00%, 4.50%)

Source: Author (2020).

Cash Flow Projections and Decision Criteria

Classical DCF Analysis

Based on the information of the fourth section, the investment feasibility of the direct real estate asset is evaluated according to two criteria—namely, the net present value on equity (NPV_e) and the internal rate of return on equity (IRR_e) as represented by equations (4.20) and (4.21).

$$NPV_e = \sum_{t=1}^{n} \frac{ATFC_t}{(1+K_e)^t} + \left[\frac{ATER_n}{(1+K_e)^n} - I_0 \right] \quad (4.20)$$

$$0 = \sum_{t=1}^{n} \frac{ATFC_t}{(1+IRR_e)^t} + \left[\frac{ATER_n}{(1+IRR_e)^n} - I_0 \right] \quad (4.21)$$

, where ATCF = after-tax cash flow;
ATER = after-tax equity reversion;
K_e = required rate of return on investment;
n = investment holding period in year;
I_0 = initial equity outlay.

The results show a positive NPV of S$5,563,288 and an IRR of 10.9 per cent, which is greater than expected return of 9 per cent. Therefore, the project is acceptable based on the classical DCF analysis.

The Fuzzy DCF Analysis

There are basically three steps involved in the imputations of the fuzzy NPV. First, the projected fuzzy cash flow for n_i holding period, where i = {1,2,3,4,5,6}, is discounted at a fuzzy expected rate of return. The fuzzy NPVs for the respective n_i period are then imputed as the fuzzy summation of the discounted fuzzy cash flow using equation (4.22), which is rewritten as follows:

$$NPV(\overline{A},n) = \overline{A}_0 \oplus \sum_{i=1}^{n} PV_{k(i)}(\overline{A}_i, i) \qquad (4.22')$$

The results of the fuzzy NPVs for n_i holding periods are summarised in table 3.

Table 3. Fuzzy net present value for ni holding periods

Holding Periods n_i Year	Fuzzy Net Present Value
1	(-21,858,120/-18,627,063, -7,499,001/-3,987,539)
2	(-22,257,317/-14,667,544, +1,282,604/+8,105,296)
3	(-23,318,025/-12,145,522, +8,739,897/+18,852,075)
4	(-24,870,682/-10,026,734, +16,587,183/+30,186,131)
5	(-26,866,944/-8,533,056, +23,269,346/+40,255,209)
6	(-29,217,232/-7,592,921, +28,901,578/+49,164,868)

As the holding periods $\overline{n}_i$ is a collection of positive discrete fuzzy numbers with a possibility distribution given in table 1, the second step involves the estimation of the membership function for the fuzzy NPV at each n_i, taking into consideration the cut-off level of λ_i. The minimum fuzzy sets are determined by the membership function below:

$$\mu(x\mid \bar{A},n_i) = \min\left[\mu(x\mid \bar{A},n_i),\lambda_i\right] \qquad (4.23)$$

Assuming that $f_1(y\mid NPV)$ and $f_2(y\mid NPV)$ are two monotonous linear functions, the intersection points (x_1, x_2) between the $\mu(x\mid \bar{A}, n_i)$ and λ_i are calculated as

$$x_1 = f_1(y\mid NPV) = (NPV_2 - NPV_1)*y + NPV_1 \qquad (4.24a)$$

$$x_2 = f_2(y\mid NPV) = (NPV_3 - NPV_4)*y + NPV_4 \qquad (4.24b)$$

After determining the fuzzy $NPV(\bar{A}, n_i)$(table 3) and their respective membership functions, the last step involves the fuzzy aggregation of the membership functions of the fuzzy NPVs from period n_1 to n_6 based on equation (19), to form the fuzzy decision space shown in figure 4.2.

$$\mu(x\mid \bar{A}) = \max_{1\le i\le k}\left[\min(\mu(x\mid \bar{A},n_i),\lambda_i)\right] \qquad (4.25)$$

The cut-off points x_i in figure 4, where i = {2,3,4,5,6,7,8}, are calculated based on equation (23). However, for point x_1 that lies on the intersection of segments $f_1(y\mid NPV_1)$ and $f_1(y\mid NPV_6)$, the determination of the height of $\mu(x\mid \bar{A})$ and the cut-off NPV requires simultaneous solving of equations (4.26) and (4.27) below:

$$f_1(y\mid NPV_1) = S\$3{,}231{,}057 \star y - S\$21{,}858{,}120 \qquad (4.26)$$

$$f_1(y\mid NPV_6) = S\$21{,}624{,}311 \star y - S\$29{,}217{,}232 \qquad (4.27)$$

The height of the membership function (y) so obtained is 0.4, and the x_1 is estimated as -S$20,565,697.

The fuzzy solution space as defined by figure 4.4 has complex membership characteristics. The ordinary investor may not find it comfortable to interpret the results in the fuzzy forms. Therefore, a 'defuzzification' process is conducted based on the 'Centroid' method

(Reynolds et al. 1973). The 'defuzzified' NPV gives an optimal non-fuzzy solution of S$8,532,785. The positive non-fuzzy value suggests the acceptance of the investment.

Fig. 4.4. The decision space of the fuzzy solution

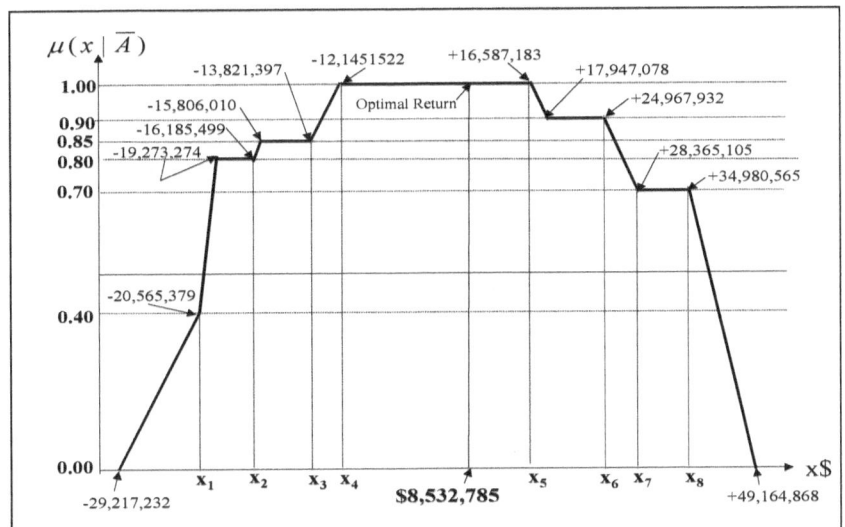

Source: Author (2020).

It is expected that the non-fuzzy result of the fuzzy DCF model will be higher than that of the classical model because of the uncertainty involved in the fuzzy solution. The variance between the fuzzy NPV of S$8,532,785 and the traditional discounted NPV of S$5,563,288 is found to be S$2,909,497 or +53.8 per cent. The finding is partly attributable to the trade-off involved in generalising the classical model and the assumption of uncertainty. Such finding is partly attributable to the significant margin of variance that is dependent on the subjective expert judgements. The findings reflect a higher degree of optimism in the transformation of the approximate estimates to the respective fuzzy numbers.

Concluding Remarks

In a highly volatile world, the best point estimate of the classical DCF model is no longer a reliable indication of the investment worth. The investment evaluation becomes outdated or obsolete rapidly as the state of the direct real estate market (DREM) changes. Many sophisticated forecasting techniques have been proposed and advanced to consolidate the variances. These techniques are criticised for generating inconsistent outcomes when the DREM is not so a random walk. Therefore, the expert experiences and market knowledge appear to be better substitutes for those quantitative methodologies in an attempt to outguess the DREM performance. The translation of these expert experiences and judgements into reliable market forecasts suffers from some limitations. Imprecision and vagueness are major obstacles to the application of expert knowledge. Incorporation of 'fuzzy set theory' to the classical models is proposed as a way to overcome the problems of fuzziness.

The fuzzy DCF model provides a natural and intuitive way of dealing with cognitive uncertainty. It relaxes the precision and crispness imposed on a rigid model, for an inexact and vague but robust representation of DREM knowledge. Investors and analysts are consequently not restrained to make imprecise but reliable predictions and relieving them of adopting data-intensive statistical analyses. Based on a set of fuzzy inputs, the fuzzy NPV can be imputed to provide an approximated evaluation of the investment interest. With the membership characteristics of the fuzzy NPVs, the uncertainty of each outcome is concurrently captured and reflected. Such a fuzzy NPV approximative model merges two limbs of investment analysis—the return and risk evaluation.

In the case illustrations, the NPV of the classical DCF model based on crisp and precise inputs is estimated at S$5,563,288. When the input variables are fuzzified with different possibility distributions, the fuzzy NPV post the centroid defuzzification process gives an optimal value of S$8,532,785. A comparison of the results shows that an increase in NPV of 53.38 per cent is obtained by the fuzzy DCF vis-à-vis the classical NPV. The implication is the assumption of greater uncertainties in the fuzzy DCF analysis. The gap between the fuzzy DCF and the classical NPV is partly attributable to the trade-off in generalising the classical model and the assumption of uncertainty. However, the gap also reflects a higher degree of optimism in the transformation of approximate estimates to the respective fuzzy numbers. Cognitive uncertainty has long been overlooked in the past. As the DREM moves away from randomness, the ability to deal with this form of uncertainty ultimately distinguishes the more viable and savvy investors. The application of the fuzzy DCF offers a competitive edge to the enlightened investor.

Acknowledgement: *The author wishes to gratefully acknowledge the initial work conducted for chapter 4 by Prof (Dr) Sing Tien Foo, head of the Department of Real Estate in the NUS School of Design and Environment, in consultation with honorary professor (University of Hertfordshire, Hatfield, UK) (Dr) Ho, Kim Hin / David; during their meaningful brainstorming sessions before Professor Ho retired from the NUS SDE Departments of Real Estate and Building in May 2019.*

References

Buckley, J. J. 1987. 'The Fuzzy Mathematics of Finance'. *Fuzzy Sets and Systems* 21: 257–273.

Dubois, D. and H. Parade. 1979. 'Fuzzy Real Algebra—Some Results'. *Fuzzy Sets and System* 2: 327–348.

Fischhoff, B. 1989. 'Eliciting Knowledge for Analytical Representations'. *IEEE Transactions on Systems, Man and Cybernetics* 19: 98–99.

Gupta, M. M. 1977. 'Fuzzy-ism', The First Decade. In Gupta, M. M., G. N. Saridis, and B. R. Gaines (eds.), *Fuzzy Automata and Decision Processes*. Elsevier North-Holland. pp. 5–10.

Klir, G. F. and T. A. Folger. 1992. *Fuzzy Sets, Uncertainty and Information*. Prentice Hall, International Edition.

Ho, K. H./D. and C. K. L. Shun. 2014. *Direct and Indirect Investment Analysis—an Asian Real Estate Perspective*. McGraw-Hill Education (Asia).

Ho, K. H./D. 2007. *International Real Estate—Asia's Potential from a Research Perspective*, NUS Press Ltd/SUP.

Makridakis, S. and S. C. Wheelwright (eds.). 1979. 'Forecasting the future and the future of forecasting'. In *Managerial Sciences: Vol. 12, Forecasting*. Amsterdam: North Holland.

Reynolds, T. J., L. E. Kent, and D. W. Lazenby. 197. *Introduction to Structural Mechanics*. London: Hodder and Stoughton.

Von Winterfeldt, D. and W. Edward. 1986. *Decision Analysis and Behavioural Research*. New York, Cambridge University Press.

Zadeh, L. A. 1977. 'Fuzzy Set Theory—a Perspective'. In Gupta, Madan M., George N. Saridis, and Brian R. Gaines (eds.), *Fuzzy Automata and Decision Processes*, Elsevier North-Holland, pp. 3–4.

CHAPTER 5

EXAMINING FUZZY TACTICAL ASSET ALLOCATION (FTAA) AS AN ALTERNATIVE TO MODERN PORTFOLIO THEORY (MPT) ASSET ALLOCATION FOR INTERNATIONAL AND DIRECT REAL ESTATE INVESTMENT

The modern portfolio theory asset allocation framework (MPTAAF) can be adopted to enable decision-making in international direct real estate investing. Often, institutional investors and direct real estate asset project managers adopt MPTAAF to support their international direct real estate investment decision-making. The MPTAAF can be enhanced to capture instead the multicausal factors influencing international direct real estate investing. A fuzzy decision-making approach is a more intuitive and rigorous alternative to the MPTAAF regard. Chapter 5 is concerned with the model formation and estimation of a unique fuzzy tactical asset allocation (FTAA), which, in turn, comprises the FTAA flexible programming and the FTAA robust programming models. Both such FTAA models enhance the classical Markowitz MPT portfolio theory on asset allocation by making it more intuitively appropriate for decision-making in international and direct real estate investing.

Direct real estate investing is envisaged to be a complex human cognitive process involving decision-making, concerning possible uncertain future total returns. The investment analysis comprises several key analytical techniques—namely, the discounted cash flow model, portfolio theory, and risk analysis, which are essentially structured frameworks that enable a more precise and certain evaluation of a direct real estate investment. However, the success of investment analysis still relies on the reliability and quality of the inputs to the analytical techniques. There are several motivations for this chapter, and for investment analysis, the precise and 'crisp' result of any of its models is derived on the assumption that the variables in the analysis are deterministic or probabilistic in nature. This assumption is pseudo-accurate, and it fails to take into account unexpected shocks or perturbations that are possible in the real world. Therefore, investors who rely on sophisticated analytical techniques are not placed in a better position but are in fact subject to substantial risk. However, expert judgement offers an acceptable alternative to non-naïve models, as that judgement, itself limited by uncertainty, is attributable to the vagueness and imprecision inherent to the associated expert's *ex ante* information. Such a limitation is known as cognitive uncertainty or fuzziness.

'Fuzzy set theory' is incepted to allow a natural and intuitive way of representing cognitive uncertainty. Fuzzy set theory relaxes the crispness and precision to enable a robust summary of expert knowledge. The incorporation of fuzzy set theory has made significant inroads relating to the generalisation of traditional asset investment analysis and its techniques, thereby opening a new frontier in structured frameworks for evaluating the direct real estate investment market. There has been a significant amount of studies focused on the potential benefits of an international direct real estate investment strategy. The diversification benefits of international direct real estate investment have been instrumental for teeming studies, but the adoption of the mean variance, Markowitz modern portfolio theory (MPT) framework has been questioned by researchers. Worzala (1992), Chenah, Ziobrowski, and Caines (1999) well agree on the lack of high-quality data on direct international real estate markets and their past performance. Given the broad nature of the direct international real estate markets' performance, it is understandably hard to find reliable data sources for major direct real estate markets that are appropriate for enabling meaningful comparison with one another. Many studies focus on the best data that is available. A pertinent question is, what proportion of capital should institutional investors and asset project managers devote to direct and international real estate investments that are subject to uncertainty? There are still puzzles in the asset allocation problem of international direct real estate investing. Such puzzles cannot be easily resolved without better data for the international direct real estate markets. Then and only then can more rigorous analysis be conducted to enable the benefits of geographical diversification, direct real estate sector diversification, and time diversification (time being one of the key sources of risk or uncertainty). Such diversification benefits are well documented by Goetzmann and Ibbotson (1990).

Chapter 5 addresses a set of short-term tactical asset allocation models, collectively known as fuzzy tactical asset allocation (FTAA)—namely, the 'FTAA Flexible Programming Model' and the 'FTAA Robust Programming Model'. Both such models apply fuzzy set theory to improve the traditional mean variance, Markowitz modern portfolio theory (MPT) framework for efficient decision-making by institutional investors and asset project managers in international and direct real estate investment. Such two FTAA programming models show a wider spread of tactical allocation weights, relative to the MPT TAA (tactical asset allocation) model portfolio that has more 0 per cent allocation weights, thereby reflecting intuitively greater geographical diversification, from a decision-making investor's perspective, amongst the ten Asian office markets for the short-term pan-Asia office TAA portfolio. All three TAA models—that is, the FTAA flexible programming model, FTAA robust programming model, and MPT TAA model, are able to achieve optimal risk-adjusted total returns (TRs) at the portfolio level via quadratic optimisation. However, the MPT TAA model is highly sensitive to estimation errors, while the precision and reliability of its estimated inputs are critical to the success of its optimisation decision. Determination of input variables that relies on historical (*ex post*) data is increasingly unreliable for forecasting (*ex ante*) purposes, in view of the refutation of the random walk hypothesis for the common stock and direct real estate markets. *Ex ante* data specifically takes into account expected movements of direct real estate markets in the short term, which represent the tactical tilts of a short-term TAA portfolio from its long-term strategic asset allocation portfolio (SAA or the policy portfolio). Hence, incorporating fuzzy set theory with the Markowitz MPT quadratic programming model enables the short-term TAA portfolio to become more intuitive FTAA programming models, which constitute uniquely natural ways of capturing *ex ante* data of the investor—and asset project manager—expert judgement of international direct real estate markets. Fuzzy approaches to asset allocation optimisation achieve the twofold benefits of risk diversification and effective risk management. Results of the estimation exercise show that the standard deviation of the office portfolio returns ranges not more than 5.70 per cent, as reflected in the two FTAA programming models.

As a result, chapter 5 is structured in several sections, starting with the introduction and followed by the related literature on asset allocation. The next (third) section discusses the two key FTAA models, and the data is subsequently discussed. The results and comparisons of the models are accordingly analysed, while the concluding remarks section closes chapter 5.

Related Literature

In general, asset allocation in finance theory refers to the process of securing the most favourable return and risk trade-off, involving competing interests that are concerned with risk reduction and return enhancement at the portfolio level but subject to various constraints (Kritzman 1992). The importance of asset allocation in arriving at optimal investing decision-making cannot be overstated (Brinson, Hood, and Beebower 1986; Grieger 1987; and Ankrim 1987). Traditionally, the asset allocation decision is based on expected mean variance theory (EMV), wherein the return and risk profile at the portfolio level has to be balanced and subject to constraints (Markowitz 1952). Recent studies have increasingly criticised the effectiveness and appropriateness of the EMV theoretical approach. A frequent criticism is the sensitivity of the results to estimation errors (Chopra and Ziemba [8]). Other commentators have highlighted its sensitivity to time factors (Kritzman 1990) and to fundamental factors (Benari 1990). The traditional way to adopt risk and return for making investment decisions is through portfolio theory. Earlier portfolio theory is based on the assumption that portfolio diversification reduces portfolio risk. Most studies in this area and the subsequent development of the capital asset pricing model (CAPM) have related to investment in the common stock market equities. However, the CAPM is not solely confined to common stock market investment but can be applied to all risky assets. Nowadays, almost all institutional investors adopt CAPM.

The Markowitz Modern Portfolio Theory (MPT)

The pioneering work of Markowitz (1959) has resulted in a radical reappraisal of the way that investors and asset project managers behave, and this pioneering work has led the way for the development of what became known as capital market theory. By defining a portfolio of assets in terms of their risk, return, and covariance, Markowitz developed a model that can identify the optimal proportion of funds to be held of each asset. For a given level of risk, the resulting portfolio is considered efficient because it offers the maximum expected return. The alternative approach is to minimise risk for a given rate of TR. Under MPT, the optimisation for the traditional asset allocation process concerning the asset portfolio can be modelled as a quadratic programming function in equation (5.1), consisting of a risk minimisation objective (G) and a few constraints (C) as follows:

$$\begin{aligned} \text{Minimize} \quad & G(x) = \sum_{i=1}^{N}\sum_{j=1}^{N} x_i x_j \sigma_{ij} \\ \text{Subject to} \quad & \\ & C_1(x_i) = \sum_{i=1}^{N} x_i \overline{R}_i - \overline{R}_P \\ & C_2(x_i) = \sum_{i=1}^{N} x_i - 1 \\ & x_i \geq 0, \quad i = 1, 2, \ldots, N \end{aligned}$$

(5.1)

, where x_i is the proportion of portfolio allocated to asset i, $\overline{R}_P$ refers to the expected portfolio return, $\overline{R}_i$ is the expected return on asset i, σ_{ij} represents the covariance between asset i returns and asset j returns, and σ_{ii} is the variance of asset i.

On MPT's shortcomings, previous studies find that the sensitivity of the input parameters adds an estimation risk to the implementation of the model. Benari (1990) highlights the sensitivity of the optimal portfolio to changes in fundamental factors like the business cycle, resource utilisation, productivity of capital, inflation, and interest rate volatility. Further and Wainscott (1990) examine the correlation of the historical and future correlations from 1925 to 1988 and find that the historical correlation of common stocks and bonds has been an unsatisfactory predictor of future correlations. Another shortcoming of the Markowitz MPT optimisation model is that such an optimiser receives insufficient attention. The optimiser comprises a set of decision rules, ranging in complexity from a simple rule of thumb to a full-scale quadratic program (Sharpe 1987). It is prone to estimation error leading to the overweighting of an asset with an overestimated return and an underestimated risk. Furthermore, the crisp and fixed goal and constraints in the optimiser further render its application rigid and are sometimes unrealistic. In Markowitz's MPT optimisation model, the 'crisp' constrained function must be strictly complied with. As a result, when more asset classes are included in the optimisation programming, then negative coefficients for asset weights may be obtained. The investor will then be compelled to sell short his assets to maintain portfolio optimality.

Fuzzy Set Theory

The uncertainty and imprecision in the application of the non-intuitive Markowitz MPT optimisation model has discouraged many investment and asset project managers who simply disregard the results or reject the entire approach right away (Michaud 1989). The degree of uncertainty is denoted as fuzziness. Therefore, the 'fuzzy set theory' is a generalisation of conventional set theory, developed by Zadeh (1965) as a mathematical way of representing vagueness in everyday life. The development of this theory to fuzzy technology during the last forty years has advanced in many disciplines. Application of this theory can be found in many areas, such as artificial intelligence, computer science, decision theory, and expected system logic.

Fuzzy set theory simplifies complexity by increasing the amount of allowable uncertainty through sacrificing some of the precise information in favour of a vague but robust summary (Klir and Folger 1992). Fuzzy set theory is advocated by Zadeh, and most fuzzy decision theories are straightforward extensions of the corresponding conventional theories. Like mathematics, fuzzy set theory is merely a language that is adopted to fuzzify a theoretical proposition (Kickert 1978). It can be generalised to deal with problems in a fuzzy environment—that is, one that has uncertainty, imprecision, vagueness, or a poorly defined problem; in short, fuzziness. In this regard, expert judgement can be represented by fuzzy sets.

Fuzzy Optimisation

In reality, the environment in which decision-making takes place is in fact fuzzy because the decision maker is confronted with goals and constraints that cannot be precisely defined. Uncertainty of the consequences of an action rises because the interaction between the goal and the constraint functions has been blurred. This problem can be overcome by making use of fuzzy decision, as advocated by Bellman and Zadeh (1970), whereby optimisation is viewed as an operation comprising the intersection of goals and constraints, precisely defined in a fuzzy space.

Fuzzy Decision

Decision-making in a fuzzy environment is envisaged by Bellman and Zadeh to be a fuzzy decision, defined as that fuzzy set of alternative space resulting from the intersection of fuzzy goals and fuzzy constraints to achieve the 'confluence of goals and constraints'. Assume that we are given a fuzzy goal G and a fuzzy constraint C in a space of alternatives x. Then G and C combine to form a decision D that is a fuzzy set, resulting from the intersection of G and C. In symbols, $D = G \cap C$, while the fuzzy set decision is characterised by its membership function, $\mu_D = \min\{\mu_G, \mu_C\}$ wherein μ_G and μ_C are functions of x—that is, $\mu_G = \mu_G(x)$ while $\mu_C = \mu_C(x)$.

The distinguishing feature of such a fuzzy set (decision D) is its symmetry with respect to the goals and constraints, and its fuzzy set definition is modelled in figure 5.1, which forms the foundation for the development of many fuzzy mathematical programming decision-making models. In general, when n-ary goals and m-ary constraints are given, the fuzzy set decision D and its general membership function μ_D can be expressed in equation (5.2).

$$D = G_1 \cap G_2 \cap ... \cap G_n \cap C_1 \cap G_2 \cap ... \cap G_m \qquad (5.2)$$

, with $\mu_D = Min\{\mu_{Gn}, \mu_{Cm}\}$; $n, m \in N$.

Fig. 5.1. The general fuzzy set decision and membership function

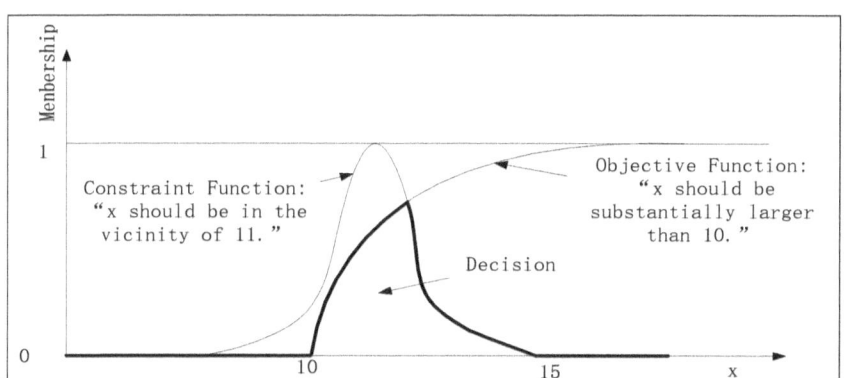

Source: Author (2020).

NB: Objective function, G (*x*), and constraint function, C(*x*), and with some example measurement of x; the bold line denotes the fuzzy decision as the intersection of G and C.

The decision space expressed as a fuzzy decision set D provides a natural solution, which is difficult to interpret directly, and should be 'defuzzified' into a non-fuzzy solution. The 'crisp', non-fuzzy decision D_m, in general, is a subset of D, known as the optimal decision. It is determined by the set with the highest degree of the membership function, whereas the element (*x*) of the subset D_m is referred to as the maximising decision in equation (5.3).

$$\mu_D(x) = Max\mu_D(x) \qquad (5.3)$$

For fuzzy decisions, the term decision can have very many different meanings, depending on whether it is used by a lawyer, a businessman, an army general, a psychologist, or a statistician.

The Fuzzy Tactical Asset Allocation (FTAA) Models

This section discusses the two key and complementary fuzzy tactical asset allocation (FTAA) models to enable decision-making for international and direct real estate investing. These models consist of the 'FTAA flexible programming model' and the 'FTAA robust programming model'. Adopting mathematical models of reality, we often encounter the problem of finding all non-negative solutions of the system of 'm' constraints in equation (3). Such a system is frequently encountered in operations research and the mathematical economy.

$$a_{i1}x_1 + a_{i2}x_2 + \ldots + a_{in}x_n \leq b_i, i = 1, \ldots, m. \quad (3)$$

The parameters a_{ij}, b_i are usually supposed to be the fixed characteristics of modelled reality. Unfortunately, real-world problems do not always benefit from this. On the contrary, the parameters are often not known exactly because they are variable, unreliable, or imprecise in a certain sense. Fuzzy approaches usually applied to such a problem may be classified into two categories: the 'flexible programming' (Negoita 1981) and the 'robust programming'. The first category, the 'flexible programming', consists of weakening the constraints of the classical optimisation problem and of reformulating it into a new one, a set of feasible solutions that are fuzzy. The concept of the optimal solution is then based on the intersection of fuzzy sets. The second category, the 'robust programming', enables problems to be modelled, whose structures are not exact, by making the imprecision of the associated parameters to be considered for the model's construction phase. The problem so resolved in this way has constraints with fuzzy parameters, where the variables x_i are non-fuzzy. Two fuzzy mathematical programming models are adopted: the FTAA flexible programming model and the FTAA robust programming model.

The FTAA flexible programming model involves a fuzzy optimiser modelled along the lines of Zimmermann's 'symmetric fuzzy linear programming' model, which consists of a fuzzy objective and a few fuzzy constraints. The FTAA robust programming model expresses the optimisation problem in the form of fuzzy coefficients. In this chapter, the fuzzy programming optimisation is conducted for the two key FTAA models within the context of the common-stock share assets in the Singapore Stock Exchange and direct real estate assets in Singapore.

FTAA Flexible Model—Zimmerman's Symmetric Fuzzy Linear Programming Model

In the classical Markowitz MPT quadratic programming optimisation, the risk minimisation objective is strictly observed, and any violation of the constraints is unacceptable, regardless of the extent of noncompliance. Such a rigid approach conflicts with real-world problem, where the decision maker may not insist on minimum risk but rather desires a tolerable level of risk. Consequently, a small violation of the constraints within the tolerance interval should not cause the decision maker to reject the feasible solution. This 'small violation' refers to the linguistic (fuzzy) explanation for vagueness. Take for instance an investor's expected return is 10 per cent, and in fuzzy set theory, we can therefore take 9 per cent or 11 per cent to be a -1 per cent or +1 per cent 'small' violation from 10 per cent. The fuzzy objective and constraints are introduced by Zimmermann (1983) in his seminal 'symmetric fuzzy linear programming' model. In this model, the 'crisp' objective and constraints functions are softened to accommodate the uncertainty in real-world problem. The basic 'fuzzy linear programming' model is adopted to construct the fuzzy optimiser for a two-asset optimisation problem. Linear programming models are be considered to be a special kind of decision model where the decision space is defined by constraints, C^T, while the 'goal' (i.e., the utility function) is defined by the objective function, $f(x)$, and the type of decision is then denoted as decision-making under certainty. The FTAA flexible model can in essence be defined by the classical model of linear programming in equation (5.4) as

Maximise $f(x) = C^T x$
such that $A x \leq b$
with $x \geq 0$
and $C, x \varepsilon R^n, b \varepsilon R^m, A \varepsilon R^{m \times n}$ (5.4)

, where A, b and C are coefficients, m is the number of constraints, n is the number of goals, and $R^{m \times n}$ is the $m \times n$ real matrix.

Let us now depart from the classical assumptions that all the coefficients of A, b, and C are crisp numbers, and that the symbol $\leq$ is meant to be in a crisp sense and that 'maximise' is a strict imperative. A number of possible modifications to equation (5.4) can exist. First of all, the decision maker may want to reach some aspiration levels that may not be crisply defined. The Bellman-Zadeh concept of a symmetrical decision model of equation (5.2) should be adopted in this case. Second, the constraints can be vague—that is, the $\leq$ sign is not_meant to be taken in a strictly mathematical sense but that smaller violations may well be acceptable. One has to decide how the term known as fuzzy 'maximise' is to be interpreted or whether to stick to a crisp 'maximise'. Finally, the role of the constraints can be different from that in the classical non-fuzzy LP model, where the decision maker not only may well accept small violations of constraints but may also attach different degrees of importance to the violations of different constraints. One has to decide where and how fuzziness enters the constraints. Some authors (Tanaka and Asai 1984) deem the coefficients of A, b, and C to be fuzzy numbers and the constraints as fuzzy functions.

In the above approaches, one has to decide the type of membership function characterising either the fuzzy numbers or the fuzzy sets, representing goal and constraints. In contrast to the classical non-fuzzy LP, the 'fuzzy linear programming' is not a crisply defined type of model. Many variations are possible, depending on the assumptions or features or the real situation to be modelled. A first basic model for 'fuzzy linear programming' is shown below. We shall assume that the decision maker can establish an aspiration level, z, for the value of the objective function he wants to achieve, and that each of the constraints is modelled as a fuzzy set. Our fuzzy LP then becomes equation (5.5) in the following manner:

Find x such that
$C^T \gtrsim z$
$A x \lesssim b$
$x \geq 0$
with $C, x \varepsilon R^n, b \varepsilon R^m, A \varepsilon R^{m \times n}$ (5.5)

, where C is the objective function, A is the constraint function, z is the aspiration level, m is the number of constraints, n is the number of goals, and $R^{m \times n}$ is the $m \times n$ real matrix. The symbols $\gtrsim$ and $\lesssim$ denote the fuzzified versions of $\geq$ and $\leq$, respectively, and they have the linguistic interpretation of 'essentially greater than and equal' and of 'essentially smaller than or equal'. Since the n-vector x is variable symmetric to both the objective and constraint functions, their coefficients can be substituted by $\binom{-C}{A} = B$ and $\binom{-z}{b} = d$. Then equation (5.6) can be simplified as

find x such that $Bx \lesssim d$
$x \geq 0$
$B \varepsilon R^{(m+1) \times n}, x \varepsilon R^n, d \varepsilon R^{(m+1)}$ (5.6)

, where d is a new matrix ($d \varepsilon R^{m+1}$), formed from matrix b and aspiration level z. If each of the (m+1) rows is considered as a fuzzy function, with membership functions of $\mu_i(x)$, $i = 1, ...,m+1$, being so assigned, then the membership functions $\mu_i(x)$ are assumed to be linear, to be increasing monotonically from 0 to 1 over the tolerance interval $[d_i, d_i + P_i]$, such that

$$\mu_i(x) = \begin{cases} 1 & \text{if } (Bx)_i \leq d_i \\ 1 - \dfrac{(Bx)_i - d_i}{p_i} & \text{if } d_i \prec (Bx)_i \leq d_i + p_i \\ 0 & \text{if } (Bx)_i \succ d_i + p_i \end{cases} \qquad (5.7)$$

for $i = 1, \ldots, m+1$.

The p_i are constants subjectively chosen to represent the admissible violation of the constraint and objective functions. The fuzzy decision according to the Bellman and Zadeh model of equation (5.2) can be written after some rearrangement (see Zimmermann 1983).

$$D(x) = \min_{i=1}^{m+1} \left\{ 1 - \frac{(Bx)_i - d_i}{p_i} \right\} \qquad (5.8)$$

The crisp optimal solution will be defined along the formulation of equation (5.3) as

$$D^m(x_0) = \max_{x \geq 0} \min_{i=1}^{m+1} \left\{ 1 - \frac{(Bx)_i - d_i}{p_i} \right\} \qquad (5.9)$$

Introducing the fuzzy set decision corresponding to equation (5.7) as a new variable λ, equation (5.6) can be written as

Maximise λ
such that $\lambda p_i + (Bx)_i \leq d_i + p_i, = 1, \ldots, m+1$

$$\lambda \geq 0$$
$$x \geq 0 \qquad (5.10)$$

The maximising solution x in equation (8) can be found by solving a standard linear programming problem with an additional variable and an additional constraint.

The Fuzzy Optimiser

In a two-asset model, the classical optimiser can be generalised to include a fuzzy objective and several fuzzy constraints. Modelled along Zimmermann's fuzzy LP, the fuzzy optimiser is constructed in equation (5.11).

Maximise λ subject to constraints (5.11)

$$\lambda p_1 + \sigma_s^2 W_s^2 + \sigma_r^2 W_r^2 + 2Cor(\sigma_s, W_s)(\sigma_r, W_r) \leq Inf\{\sigma_s, \sigma_r\} + p_1$$
$$\lambda p_2 + R_s W_s + R_r W_r \leq Sup\{R_s, R_r\} + p_2$$
$$-\lambda p_3 + W_s + W_r \geq 1 - p_3$$
$$\lambda, Ws, Wr \geq 0$$

, where the spread of the tolerance intervals is given as

$$P_1 = Sup\{\sigma_s, \sigma_r\} - Inf\{\sigma_s, \sigma_r\}$$
$$P_2 = Sup\{R_s, R_r\} - Inf\{R_s, R_r\}$$
$$P_3 = 0.5$$

W denotes the allocation weights of assets s and r, while the symbols R_s, R_r, Inf, Sup are explained below.

As the first constraint function of equation (5.11) aims at minimising the portfolio risk, the aspiration level z should be the upper bound, expressed as the infermun (Inf) of σ_s or σ_r. The second constraint of equation (5.11) places a ceiling on the weighed return of the combined assets, specified as the return of the individual asset, either asset s or r, whichever is higher. Alternatively, the weighted return can be constrained by the minimum return, which is represented by the infermun (Inf) of the individual asset return, either asset s or r (Inf{Rs,Rr}). Since the objective is to minimise risk, the constraint should opt for the highest possible portfolio return. Therefore, the supremun (Sup) is used in this model. Following the expected mean variance principle, the combination of two assets, which are not perfectly correlated, reduces the portfolio risk to a level somewhere between the risk levels of the two assets. The portfolio return is also to be somewhere between the returns of the two assets. Therefore, the tolerance interval for each of the first two expressions of the equation (5.11)—that is, (p_1) and (p_2)—are then used as constraints to represent the admissible violation of the constraint and objective functions. The third expression of equation (5.11) simply implies that the uninvested portfolio is disallowed because the short sale of any asset is undesirable. However, the investor may wish to accept a larger allocation weight, say, up to 50 per cent of the portfolio composition.

FTAA Robust Model—Ramik and Rimanek's Robust Programming Model

Different approaches to generalise the crisp coefficients of model have been proposed by several researchers: Tanaka and Asai (1984); Ramik and Rimanek (1985); Chanas (1989); Delgado, Verdegay, and Vila (1989); Rommelfanger (1989); Negoita (1981); Luhardjula (1989); and Sakawa and Yano (1991). In this section, the Ramik and Rimanek's fuzzy linear programming model with fuzzy parameters is adopted because of its computational efficiency and because it expediently utilises left-right (L-R) fuzzy numbers (Dubolis and Prade 1980). The FTAA robust model of Ramik and Rimanek's optimisation problem is defined by equation (5.12) as maximising (minimising) the real function of n real variables,

$$f(x_1, x_2, ..., x_n) \tag{5.12}$$

subject to

$$\tilde{a}_{i1} x_1 \oplus \tilde{a}_{i2} x_2 \oplus \cdots \oplus \tilde{a}_{in} x_n \leq \tilde{b}_i$$
$$i = 1, \cdots, m$$
$$x_j \geq 0, j = 1, \cdots, n$$

, with $\tilde{a}_{ij} \& \tilde{b}_i \in M_{LI-Ri}$ being fuzzy numbers of left-right (L-R) type introduced by Dubuis and Prade (1980). The symbol $\oplus$ denotes the extended addition. For two L-R fuzzy numbers

$\tilde{a}_{ij} = (m_{ij}, n_{ij}, \alpha_{ij}, \beta_{ij})$ & $\tilde{b} = (p_i, q_i, \gamma_i, \delta_i)$, they assert that $\tilde{a} \leq \tilde{b}$ is valid if the following four inequalities hold:

$$\varepsilon_L(\gamma - \alpha) \leq p - m$$
$$\varepsilon_R(\beta - \delta) \leq q - n$$
$$\delta_L(\gamma - \alpha) \leq p - m$$
$$\delta_R(\beta - \delta) \leq q - n \qquad (5.13)$$

, where the above fuzzy numbers are defined as:

$$\varepsilon_R = \sup\{u; R(u) = R(0) = 1\}$$
$$\delta_R = \inf\{u; R(u) = \lim_{s \to +\infty} R(s)\} \qquad (5.14)$$

and

$$\varepsilon_L = \sup\{u; L(u) = L(0) = 1\}$$
$$\delta_L = \inf\{u; L(u) = \lim_{s \to +\infty} L(s)\} \qquad (5.15)$$

For symmetric fuzzy number $\tilde{a}, \tilde{b} \,\varepsilon M_{L-L}$ where $\tilde{a} = (m, m, \alpha, \alpha)$ and $b = (p, p, \gamma, \gamma)$, the inequalities in equation (5.13) can be reduced to the two inequalities of equation (16).

$$\varepsilon_L |\alpha - \gamma| \leq p - m$$
$$\delta_L |\alpha - \gamma| \leq p - m \qquad (5.16)$$

Applying Lemma 1 as defined in the Ramik and Rimanek chapter, the extended operation of the product of the product of the fuzzy numbers and variable x of the constraint function is given by equation (5.17):

$$a_{i1}x_1 \oplus a_{i2}x_2 \oplus \cdots \oplus a_{in}x_n = (\sum_{j=1}^{n} m_{ij}x_i \bullet \sum_{j=1}^{n} n_{ij}x_j \bullet \sum_{j=1}^{n} \alpha_{ij}x_j \bullet \sum_{j=1}^{n} \beta_{ij}x_j) \qquad (5.17)$$

From equation (5.17), the constraint function can be written in equation (18) as

$$-\varepsilon_{Li}(\sum_{j=1}^{n}\alpha_{ij}x_j - \gamma_i) \leq p_i - \sum_{j=1}^{n}m_{ij}x_j$$

$$-\delta_{Li}(\sum_{j=1}^{n}\alpha_{ij}x_j - \gamma_i) \leq p_i - \sum_{j=1}^{n}m_{ij}x_j$$

$$\varepsilon_{Ri}(\sum_{j=1}^{n}\beta_{ij}x_j - \delta_i) \leq q_i - \sum_{j=1}^{n}n_{ij}x_j$$

$$\delta_{Ri}(\sum_{j=1}^{n}\beta_{ij}x_j - \delta_i) \leq q_i - \sum_{j=1}^{n}n_{ij}x_j \tag{5.18}$$

The Data

Reliable data is required to make the FTAA models valid. *Ex ante* data from Jones Lang LaSalle (JLL) is utilised, as JLL is a leading global provider of integrated real estate and money management services, in particular its Singapore-based JLL Real Estate Intelligence Service-Asia (JLL REIS-Asia). It serves clients locally and regionally from offices in more than a hundred markets across five continents. Working from three geographic regions—the Americas, Asia Pacific, and Europe—JLL provides management, transaction, and advisory services to real estate owners, occupiers, and investors. Prime office annual total returns (TRs) are obtained for the ten Asia real estate markets—namely, Beijing, Shanghai, Seoul, Tokyo, Hong Kong (the central and major business districts), Manila (Makati CBD), Jakarta, Singapore (the Raffles Place CBD), Kuala Lumpur, and Bangkok. The TR[3] data set spans the period from 2000 to 2005 in

---

[3] TRs measure the returns to investment by combining the rental income and CV growth. Similar to the computation of yields, no allowance is made for transactions costs in the computation of total returns. In calculating TRs (historic and forecast), we take into account: (a) initial yield: the percentage return on property investment based on current effective rental income; and (b) capital growth: the increase or decrease in the CV in the year of assessment is calculated as the capital growth component of TRs. TRs are the aggregate of the initial rental returns plus the CV appreciation in the year of assessment: (Period-on-Period ΔTRI_t) = $(CV_t - CV_{t-1})/CV_t$ + Average $(Y_t$

U.S. dollar terms. In Asia, JLL REIS-Asia is the sole service provider that maintains a reliable transaction-based set of indicators for prime office property market performance in the ten country markets of Asia. JLL REIS-Asia also produces five-year total return forecasts in local currency terms for each of the markets and several key real estate market indicators (i.e., market demand growth, completions, vacancy, rental change, yield, and capital value growth). The *ex ante* values of table 5.1 and table 5.2 are obtained from the authors' own calculations. *Ex ante* data is obtained from JLL REIS-Asia, while the standard deviation (Std. Dev.), mean, and other summary statistics are imputed. Utilisation of *ex ante* values and data is consistent with the theories of the security market line and the capital market line, where the expected return on an investment asset and being correctly priced is a positive linear function of its systematic (market-wide) risk.

Furthermore, portfolio analysis is best conducted in terms of expectations because historic (*ex post*) data only provide evidence of past performance. Therefore, *ex post* data should be adjusted to take account of market expectations before it can be used in a portfolio analysis. The Jarque-Bera (J-B) test statistics, and their high probabilities do not reject the null hypothesis of the normal distribution for the *ex ante* TRs. The TRs are more positively skewed relative to the normal distribution on the whole while having a flat distribution (platykurtic) relative to the normal. At the same time, the correlation coefficients amongst the TRs are imputed, with several negatively signed correlation coefficients involving the Shanghai (SH), Beijing (BJ), Seoul (SL), Manila (MN), Singapore (SG), Kuala Lumpur (KL), and Bangkok (BK) office sectors.

:Y_{t-1}) with TRI_0 = 100, TRI_t = [(Period-on-Period $\Delta TRIt$) + 1] x TRI_0, TRI_{t+1} = [(Period-on-Period $\Delta TRIt+1$) + 1] x TRI_t; where: TR is total returns, TRI is total returns index, CV denotes capital values, and Y denotes initial yields.

Table 5.1. Forecast (ex ante) total returns (TRs), 2006–2010

City or Country	Beijing	Shanghai	Central + Major Business Districts	Seoul	Tokyo	Manila	Jakarta	Singapore (Raffles Place)	Kuala Lumpur	Bangkok
	China	China	HK	South Korea	Japan	Philippines	Indonesia	Singapore	Malaysia	Thailand
	BJ	SH	HK	SL	TK	MN	JK	SG	KL	BK
Mean	10.88%	16.39%	3.47%	15.86%	15.17%	22.57%	16.95%	11.64%	11.75%	12.29%
Median	12.55%	17.36%	-2.02%	15.05%	8.64%	17.35%	17.53%	11.10%	11.03%	10.61%
Maximum	16.51%	21.59%	39.95%	18.44%	48.38%	42.72%	25.70%	18.11%	19.82%	20.11%
Minimum	2.28%	12.37%	-26.85%	12.46%	-0.85%	15.34%	10.69%	6.20%	2.15%	7.96%
Std. Dev.	5.35%	3.93%	24.94%	2.56%	19.30%	11.56%	5.76%	4.98%	7.01%	5.09%
Kurtosis	2.488	1.598	2.130	1.613	2.909	2.983	2.176	1.530	1.767	2.043
J-B	0.601	0.420	0.269	0.412	1.248	1.458	0.379	0.485	0.347	0.622
Probability	0.740	0.810	0.874	0.814	0.536	0.482	0.828	0.785	0.841	0.733

Source: JLL Real Estate Intelligence Service Asia, JLL REIS Asia, data and forecasts (2007); author (2020). <u>NB:</u> Std. Dev. = standard deviation.

Table 5.2. Ex-ante correlations amongst the Asian country TRs, 2006–2010

	BJ	SH	HK	SL	TK	MN	JK	SG	KL	BK
BJ	1.000	-0.458	0.081	-0.665	0.113	-0.283	0.346	-0.641	-0.766	-0.162
SH	-0.458	1.000	-0.328	0.491	0.571	0.776	0.298	0.931	0.318	0.943
HK	0.081	-0.328	1.000	-0.497	0.396	0.158	0.503	-0.267	0.358	-0.212
SL	-0.665	0.491	-0.497	1.000	-0.346	-0.097	-0.625	0.406	0.047	0.238
TK	0.113	0.571	0.396	-0.346	1.000	0.884	0.947	0.515	0.296	0.760
MN	-0.283	0.776	0.158	-0.097	0.884	1.000	0.750	0.832	0.591	0.832
JK	0.346	0.298	0.503	-0.625	0.947	0.750	1.000	0.266	0.195	0.549
SG	-0.641	0.931	-0.267	0.406	0.515	0.832	0.266	1.000	0.603	0.818
KL	-0.766	0.318	0.358	0.047	0.296	0.591	0.195	0.603	1.000	0.163
BK	-0.162	0.943	-0.212	0.238	0.760	0.832	0.549	0.818	0.163	1.000

Source: JLL Real Estate Intelligence Service Asia, JLL REIS Asia, data and forecasts (2007); author (2020).

Results of the MPT and FTAA models

The MPT Results

For the purpose of estimating the two short-run fuzzy tactical asset allocation (FTAA) models, we assume a long-term strategic asset allocation (SAA) portfolio composition, which is separately determined from another exercise deploying four factors—that is, economic growth prospects, direct real estate market liquidity, transparency, and vacancy. It is around the SAA that the linear programming optimisations of the two FTAA models are carried out. Table 5.3 presents the required SAA composition weights for the ten-city pan-Asia office portfolio. These two FTAA models denote the Zimmerman's FTAA flexible programming model (eq. [5.4] to [4.10]) and the Ramik and Rimanek FTAA robust programming model (eq. [5.12] to [5.18]). These FTAA models are subsequently discussed in the next subsections. The required *ex ante* data is presented and summarised in table 3 from which the pan-Asia office total return (TR) correlation coefficients are imputed in table 5.4, while the corresponding covariance matrix is presented in table 5.5. It is observed from this table that Shanghai has high correlations with Manila, Singapore, and Bangkok and moderate correlations with Seoul and Tokyo. The resulting Markowitz MPT optimisation model of equation (5.1) is presented as the efficient frontier of figure 5.2.

Table 5.3. The long-run strategic asset allocation (SAA) portfolio composition

	Pan-Asia Office Real Estate Sector (Market) SAA Allocation Weights					
Factors	Economic Growth Prospects	Liquidity	Market Transparency	Market Vacancy	Strategic Allocation, Index	SAA Weight
Market	EconGthPro	Mkt Liquidity	MktTransparency	Mkt Vacancy	MktPerformance	%
BJ	9	6	6	2	0.8333	15.31%
SH	9	6	6	3	0.7777	14.28%
HK	5	9	9	3	0.5	9.18%
SL	7	7	7	7	0.5833	10.71%
TK	4	7	8	6	0.5	9.18%
MN	6	6	6	6	0.5666	10.41%
JK	4	4	4	4	0.4333	7.96%
SG	4	9	9	3	0.5	9.18%
KL	5	5	5	7	0.5001	9.19%
BK	4	4	4	8	0.25	4.59%
				Total	5.4443	100%

Source: Author (2020); JLL REIS-Asia (2009); fuzzyTech5.12e software program (2010).

Table 5.4. Summarised ex ante data of the ten Asian office sectors

Office Market	Beijing	Shanghai	Central + Major Business Districts	Seoul	Tokyo	Manila	Jakarta	Singapore (Raffles Place)	Kuala Lumpur	Bangkok
Country	China	China	HK	South Korea	Japan	Philippines	Indonesia	Singapore	Malaysia	Thailand
	BJ	SH	HK	SL	TK	MN	JK	SG	KL	BK
2006	9.94%	21.59%	13.34%	15.05%	48.38%	42.72%	25.70%	18.11%	17.14%	20.11%
2007	2.28%	17.36%	-7.06%	18.44%	-0.85%	21.87%	10.69%	15.09%	19.82%	10.61%
2008	13.13%	18.08%	-26.85%	18.40%	5.91%	15.59%	12.99%	11.10%	2.15%	14.48%
2009	16.51%	12.37%	-2.02%	12.46%	8.64%	17.35%	17.83%	7.69%	8.61%	8.30%
2010	12.55%	12.54%	39.95%	14.95%	13.76%	15.34%	17.53%	6.20%	11.03%	7.96%
Mean	10.88%	16.39%	3.47%	15.86%	15.17%	22.57%	16.95%	11.64%	11.75%	12.29%
Std. Dev.	5.35%	3.93%	24.94%	2.56%	19.30%	11.56%	5.76%	4.98%	7.01%	5.09%

Source: JLL Real Estate Intelligence Service Asia, JLL REIS Asia, data and forecasts; author (2020).

Table 5.5. The Pan-Asia office total return (TR) correlation coefficients

	BJ	SH	HK	SL	TK	MN	JK	SG	KL	BK
BJ	1.00	-0.46	0.08	-0.67	0.11	-0.28	0.35	-0.64	-0.77	-0.16
SH	-0.46	1.00	-0.33	0.49	0.57	0.78	0.30	0.93	0.32	0.94
HK	0.08	-0.33	1.00	-0.50	0.40	0.16	0.50	-0.27	0.36	-0.21
SL	-0.67	0.49	-0.50	1.00	-0.35	-0.10	-0.63	0.41	0.05	0.24
TK	0.11	0.57	0.40	-0.35	1.00	0.88	0.95	0.52	0.30	0.76
MN	-0.28	0.78	0.16	-0.10	0.88	1.00	0.75	0.83	0.59	0.83
JK	0.35	0.30	0.50	-0.63	0.95	0.75	1.00	0.27	0.19	0.55
SG	-0.64	0.93	-0.27	0.41	0.52	0.83	0.27	1.00	0.60	0.82
KL	-0.77	0.32	0.36	0.05	0.30	0.59	0.19	0.60	1.00	0.16
BK	-0.16	0.94	-0.21	0.24	0.76	0.83	0.55	0.82	0.16	1.00

Source: JLL Real Estate Intelligence Service Asia, JLL REIS Asia, data and forecasts; author (2020).

Table 5.6. The Pan-Asia office TR covariance matrix

	BJ	SH	HK	SL	TK	MN	JK	SG	KL	BK
BJ	0.23%	-0.04%	0.09%	0.09%	-0.23%	-0.14%	-0.14%	-0.08%	-0.07%	0.09%
SH	-0.04%	0.21%	-0.22%	0.13%	0.05%	0.39%	0.17%	0.15%	0.02%	0.60%

HK	0.09%	-0.22%	4.98%	0.58%	0.50%	0.37%	-0.27%	-0.26%	-0.25%	1.52%
SL	0.09%	0.13%	0.58%	0.27%	0.06%	0.40%	0.06%	0.05%	-0.07%	0.84%
TK	-0.23%	0.05%	0.50%	0.06%	0.39%	0.38%	0.17%	0.07%	0.01%	0.32%
MN	-0.14%	0.39%	0.37%	0.40%	0.38%	1.07%	0.38%	0.28%	-0.02%	1.58%
JK	-0.14%	0.17%	-0.27%	0.06%	0.17%	0.38%	0.20%	0.15%	0.04%	0.40%
SG	-0.08%	0.15%	-0.26%	0.05%	0.07%	0.28%	0.15%	0.12%	0.04%	0.35%
KL	-0.07%	0.02%	-0.25%	-0.07%	0.01%	-0.02%	0.04%	0.04%	0.05%	-0.14%
BK	0.09%	0.60%	1.52%	0.84%	0.32%	1.58%	0.40%	0.35%	-0.14%	2.98%

Source: JLL Real Estate Intelligence Service Asia, JLL REIS Asia, data and forecasts; author (2020).

Figure 5.2 depicts the estimated efficient frontier of ten Asian office real estate markets. It is readily observed from figure 2 that the institutional investors can achieve between 12 per cent and 19 per cent for the pan-Asia office portfolio TR in relation to between 0.3 per cent and 6.3 per cent of the pan-Asia office portfolio risk (i.e., standard deviation). The risk taker amongst the institutional investors may therefore invest in the riskier portfolio—that is, those office portfolios on the efficient frontier with higher values of portfolio risk (standard deviation).

Fig. 5.2. Efficient frontier of the ten Asian office sectors

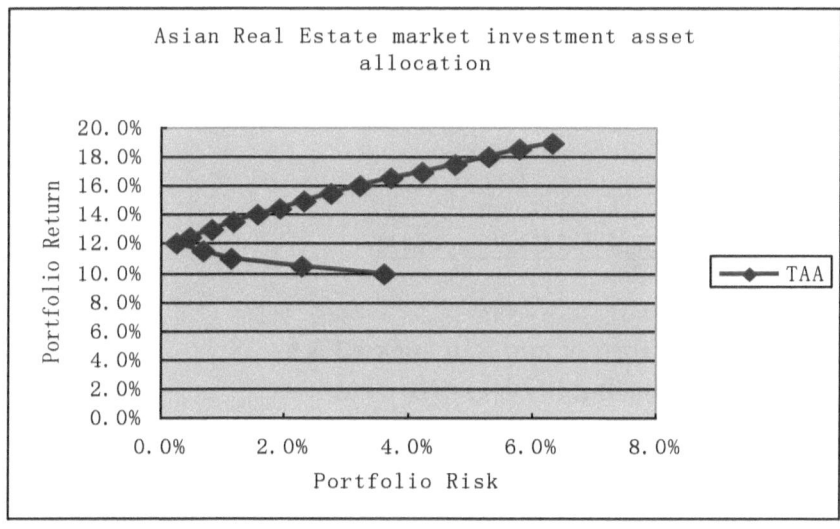

Source: Author (2020).

The FTAA Results

Estimations of the two key and short-run FTAA models of the Zimmerman FTAA flexible programming model and the Ramik and Rimanek FTAA robust programming model are summarised with their corresponding pan-Asia office portfolio weights results in tables 5.6 and 5.7 and in tables 5.8 and 5.9, respectively. Estimation details of the two models are provided in appendix C for reference.

Table 5.6. The Zimmerman FTAA flexible programming model coefficients

RISKp+λp1	18.00%	≤d1+p1	18.00%	d1	16.00%	p1	2.00%
Rp -λp2	12.00%	≥d2-p2	12.00%	d2	16.00%	p2	4.00%
Whole proportion+λp3	120.00%	≤d3+p3	120.00%	d3	100.00%	p3	20.00%

Source: Author (2020).

Table 5.7. The Zimmerman FTAA flexible programming model results

Pan-Asia Office Sectors by City	BJ	SH	HK	SL	TK	MN	JK	SG	KL	BK	λ	Total of allocation weights
Allocation Weights	1.28%	1%	3%	0%	46%	25%	4%	17%	1%	1%	1	100%
Office Portfolio Variance = 0.33%													
Office Portfolio Std. Dev. = 5.70%													
Office Portfolio Return = 16.00%													
Office Portfolio Expected Return = 16.00%													

Source: Author (2020).

Table 5.8. The Ramik and Rimanek FTAA robust programming model coefficients

Mx	14.48%	p	14.50%	εl	0.00%	_εl(αx-γ)	0.00%	≤p-mx	0.02%
Nx	16.48%	q	17.50%	δl	2.00%	_δl(αx-γ)	0.02%	≤p-mx	0.02%
αx	2.00%	γ	3.00%	εr	2.00%	εr(βx-δ)	-0.02%	≤q-nx	1.02%
βx	2.00%	δ	3.00%	δr	4.00%	δr(βx-δ)	0.00%	≤q-nx	1.02%

Source: Author (2020).

Table 9. The Ramik and Rimanek FTAA robust programming model results

Pan-Asia Office Sectors by City	BJ	SH	HK	SL	TK	MN	JK	SG	KL	BK	Total of allocation weights
Allocation Weights	0.00%	5%	0%	4%	22%	20%	7%	0%	41%	0%	100%
Office Portfolio Variance = 0.14%											
Office Portfolio Std. Dev. = 3.77%											
Office Portfolio return = 15.48%											
Office Portfolio Expected Return = 16.00%											

Source: Author (2020).

Comparison of the MPT and FTAA Models

FTAA models are essentially mere extensions of the MPT model, and they are not entirely different methods. From table 5.10, it is observed that the FTAA model portfolios both show more positive allocations relative to the MPT TAA model portfolio, which has more 0 per cent allocation weights, reflecting intuitively greater Asian city diversification in the short run. This is not to say that 0 per cent allocation weights are not good after all. In terms of portfolio risk minimisation, the FTAA robust programming model is as good as the MPT TAA model portfolio, as seen from table 5.11. All three TAA models are able to achieve optimal risk-adjusted returns at the portfolio level.

It is observed from table 5.11 that the 'flexible' and 'robust' programming models have higher portfolio risks, given the same portfolio return. It is attributable to these two FTAA models that intuitively incorporate more risk each from the decision maker (investor)'s perspective, relative to the MPT TAA model. In contrast, the quadratic programming optimisation of the MPT TAA model incorporates the risk minimisation objective that is strictly observed, and any violation of its constraints is unacceptable regardless of the extent of noncompliance—somewhat akin to corner solutions for an optimisation problem. Such a rigid approach conflicts with the real-world problem, where the investor may not insist on minimum risk but rather desires a more tolerable level of risk. Consequently, a small violation of the constraints within the tolerance interval should not cause the decision maker to reject the feasible solution. These offer plausible and intuitive explanations as to why the 'flexible' and 'robust' programming models have higher portfolio risk relative to the MPT model.

Table 5.10. Comparison of the three asset allocation models

Asia Office Markets by City			TAA	FTAA	
			Modern Portfolio Theory (MPT)	FTAA Flexible Programming Model	FTAA Robust Programming Model
Beijing	China	BJ	33.57%	1.28%	0.00%
Shanghai	China	SH	0.00%	0.83%	5.20%
Central + Major Business Districts	HK	HK	0.49%	3.01%	0.00%
Seoul	South Korea	SL	0.00%	0.50%	4.43%
Tokyo	Japan	TK	17.02%	46.16%	22.23%
Manila	Philippines	MN	0.00%	24.56%	20.18%
Jakarta	Indonesia	JK	0.00%	4.40%	6.98%
Singapore (Raffles Place)	Singapore	SG	0.00%	17.22%	0.00%
Kuala Lumpur	Malaysia	KL	48.92%	1.08%	40.98%
Bangkok	Thailand	BK	0.00%	0.95%	0.00%
	Total		100%	100%	100%

Source: Author (2020).

Table 5.11. Portfolio risk and total return (TR) comparison

	Modern Portfolio Theory (MPT)	Flexible Programming Model	Robust Programming Model
Portfolio SD	3.22%	5.70%	3.77%
Portfolio TR	16.00%	16.00%	15.48%
Expected Portfolio TR	16.00%	16.00%	16.00%

Source: Author (2020).

Concluding Remarks

The fuzzy tactical asset allocation (FTAA) model can incorporate intuitive decision-making into the asset allocation process from the perspective of the expert investor (decision maker). This FTAA model can improve the efficiency of asset allocation, adopting fuzzy set theory and fuzzy optimisation theory. The FTAA model portfolios both show more positive allocations relative to the MPT TAA model portfolio, which have more 0 per cent allocation weights, reflecting intuitively greater Asian city diversification in the short run. In terms of portfolio risk minimisation, the FTAA robust programming model is as good as the MPT TAA model portfolio from table 11. All three TAA models are able to achieve optimal risk-adjusted returns at the portfolio level. Both the Zimmerman FTAA flexible programming model and the Ramik and Rimanek FTAA robust programming model have higher portfolio risk each, given the same portfolio return. It is attributable to these two FTAA models that intuitively incorporate more risk each from the investor's perspective, relative to the MPT TAA model.

In contrast, the quadratic programming optimisation of the MPT TAA model incorporates the risk minimisation objective that is strictly observed, and any violation of its constraints is unacceptable regardless of the extent of noncompliance. Such a rigid approach conflicts with the real-world problem, where the investor and asset project manager may not insist on minimum risk but rather desire a more tolerable level of risk. Consequently, a small violation of the constraints within the tolerance interval should not cause the investor and asset project manager decision-maker to reject the feasible solution.

The MPT TAA model is essentially a quadratic programming optimisation model that is highly sensitive to estimation errors. Therefore, the precision and reliability of its estimated inputs are critical to the success of the optimisation decision. Determination of input variables relies on historical data, which is proven to be increasingly unreliable for forecasting purposes, in view of the refutation of the random walk hypothesis in the common stock and direct real estate markets. Expert investors with good market knowledge can provide reasonable estimates of returns, thereby relinquishing the reliance on data-intensive statistical approaches. Nevertheless, investor's and asset project manager's judgements are each constrained by the fact that the confidence of their judgements can be improved only at the expense of precision. This form of uncertainty, which is attributed to the vagueness of information and imprecision, can be quantified by fuzzy set theory.

Incorporating fuzzy set theory with the quadratic programming model offers investment and asset project management allocators with the more intuitive and natural way of capturing expert investor judgement in asset optimisation, in particular for international direct real estate portfolio allocation on a risk-adjusted basis. Both the Zimmerman FTAA flexible programming model and the Ramik and Rimanek FTAA robust programming model to asset optimisation are equally good alternatives relative to the MPT TAA model. Such two FTAA models achieve the twofold benefits of intuitively greater risk diversification by city or real estate sector and enable effective risk management. It is anticipated that these two short-run FTAA fuzzy models are expected to be readily accepted, and more such models are emerging as the effective extension of quadratic programming optimisation as more computable software programs of this kind become widespread.

Fuzzy approaches to optimisation, for asset allocation in the short run, have a limitation. In general, the fuzzy model exhibits the common feature of converting the equality function, under quadratic programming optimisation into inequality functions. Such inequality optimisation replaces the point solution of the MPT TAA optimisation problem (owing to the latter's rigid intersection of all functions), with a generalised or intuitive answer over a defined space of alternatives. The product of the fuzzy process with fuzzy inputs, in the form of the fuzzy outcome, is in actual fact a more natural and intuitive approach to investment and asset project management optimisation.

Acknowledgement: *The author wishes to gratefully acknowledge the initial work carried out for chapter 5 by Mr Su Hui Yong, a private real estate consultant and postgraduate (of the NUS School of Design and Environment, Department of Real Estate); and in consultation with honorary professor (University of Hertfordshire, Hatfield, UK), Dr Ho, Kim Hin / David, during their meaningful brainstorming sessions before Professor Ho retired from the NUS SDE Departments of Real Estate and Building in May 2019.*

References

Ankrim, E. M., 'Risk-Adjusted Performance Attribution'. *Financial Analysts Journal*, March/April, 1992, pp. 75–82.

Bellman, R. E., and L.A. Zadeh, 'Decision-Making in a Fuzzy Environment'. *Management Science*, 7, 1970, pp. 141–164.

Benari, Y., 'Optimal Asset Mix and its Link to Changing Fundamental Factors'. *Journal of Portfolio Management*, Winter 1990, pp. 11–18.

Brinson, G. P., L. R. Hood, and G. I. Beebower. 'Determinants of Portfolio Performance'. *Financial Analysts Journal*, July/August 1986, pp. 39–44.

Chana, S., 'Fuzzy Programming in Multiobjective Linear Programming—a Parametric Approach'. *Fuzzy Sets and Systems*, Vol. 29 (3), 1989, pp. 303–313.

Chenh, P., A. J. Ziobrowski, R. W. Caines, and B. J. Ziobrowski. 1999. 'Uncertainty and Foreign Real Estate Investing'. *Journal of Real Estate Research*, Vol. 18 No.3.

Chopra, V. K., and W. T. Ziemba. 'The Effect of Errors in Means, Variances and Covariances on Optimal Portfolio Choice'. The *Journal of Portfolio Management*, Fall 1990, pp. 6–11.

Delgado, M., J. L. Verdegay, and M. A. Vila. 'A General Model for Fuzzy Linear Programming'. *Fuzzy Sets and Systems*, Vol. 29 (1), 1989, pp. 21–29.

Dubois, D. and H. Prade. *Fuzzy Sets and Systems: Theory and Applications*. Academic Press, New York, 1980.

Grieger, D. T., 'U.S. Equity Analysis of Management Effect Description'. Frank Russell Company, Tacoma, April 1987.

Goetzmann, W. N. and R. G. Ibbotson. 'Do Winners Repeat? Patterns in Mutual Fund Behavior,' Chapters fb-_91-04, Columbia-Graduate School of Business, 1990.

Ho, K. H./D. and C. K. L. Shun. 2014. *Direct and Indirect Investment Analysis—an Asian Real Estate Perspective*. McGraw-Hill Education (Asia).

Ho, K. H./D. 2007. *International Real Estate—Asia's Potential from a Research Perspective*. NUS Press Ltd/SUP.

Klir, G. F. and T. A. Folger. *Fuzzy Sets, Uncertainty and Information*. Prentice Hall, International Edition, 1992. Kritzman, M. *Asset Allocation for Institutional Portfolios*. Richard D. Irwin Inc., 1990.

Kritzman, M. 'What Practitioners Need to Know about Optimization'. *Financial Analysts Journal*, September/October 1992, pp. 10–18.

Luhandjula, M. J. 'Fuzzy Optimization: An Appraisal'. *Fuzzy Sets and Systems*, Vol. 30, 1989, pp. 257–282.

Markowitz, Harry M. 'Portfolio Selection'. *Journal of Finance*, Vol. 7, 1952, pp. 77–91.

Michaud, R. O. 'The Markowitz Optimization Enigma: Is "Optimized" Optimal?' *Financial Analysts Journal*, January/February, 1989, pp. 31–42.

Negoita, C. V. 'The Current Interest in Fuzzy Optimization'. *Fuzzy Sets and Systems*, 6, 1981, pp. 261–269.

Ramik and Rimanek. 'Inequality Relation Between Fuzzy Numbers and Its Use In Fuzzy Optimization'. *Fuzzy Sets and Systems*, Vol. 16, No. 2, July 1985.

Rommelfanger, H., R. Hanuscheck, and J. Wolf. 'Linear Programming with Fuzzy Objectives'. *Fuzzy Sets and Systems*, Vol. 29 (1), 1989, pp. 31–48.

Sakawa, M., and H. Yano. 'Feasibility and Parato Optimality for Multiobjective Nonlinear Programming Problems with Fuzzy Parameter'. *Fuzzy Sets and Systems*, Vol. 43(1), 1991, pp. 1–15.

Sharp, W. F. 'An Algorithm for Portfolio Improvement'. *Advances in Mathematical Programming and Financial Planning*, Vol. 1, Greenwich, CT: JAI Press Inc., 1987.

Tanaka H., and K. Asai. 'Fuzzy Linear Programming Problems with Fuzzy Numbers'. *Fuzzy Sets and Systems*, Vol. 13, 1984, pp. 1–10.

Waiscott, C. B. 'The Stock-Bond Correlation and Its Implication for Asset Allocation'. *Financial Analysts Journal*, July/August, 1990, pp. 55.

Worzala, E. M. 1992. 'International Direct Real Estate Investments as Alternative Portfolio Assets for Institutional Investors: An Evaluation', unpublished PhD dissertation, University of Wisconsin-Madison.

Zaded, L. A. 'Fuzzy Sets'. *Information and Control*, 8, 1965, pp. 338–352.

Zimmermann, H. J., and P. Zysno. 'Decisions and Evaluations by Hierarchical Aggregation of Information'. *Fuzzy Sets and Systems*, Vol. 10 (3), 1983, pp. 243–260.

Appendix A. The Fuzzy Tactical Asset Allocation Models

For the fuzzy tactical asset allocation models, the most important thing is to identify all the parameters used in each model.

1. Zimmerman's FTAA flexible programming model coefficients

RISKp+λp1	18.00%	≤d1+p1	18.00%	d1	16.00%	p1	2.00%
Rp −λp2	12.00%	≥d2−p2	12.00%	d2	16.00%	p2	4.00%
Whole proportion+λp3	120.00%	≤d3+p3	120.00%	d3	100.00%	p3	20.00%

Source: Author (2020).

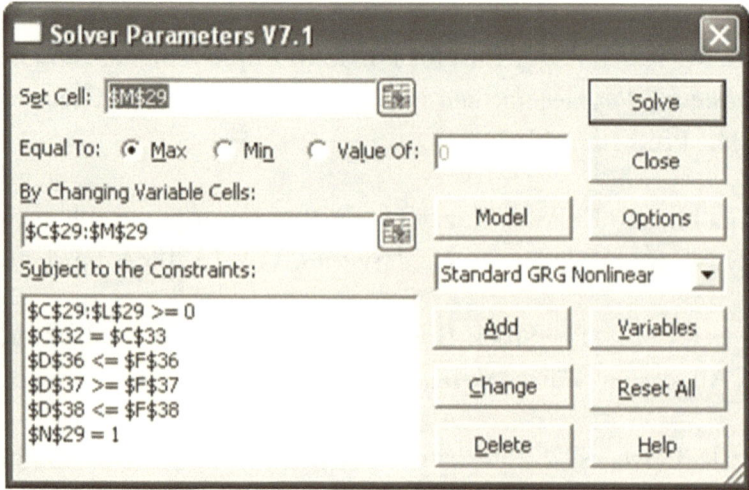

PROJECT MANAGEMENT - AN ARTIFICIAL INTELLIGENT (AI) APPROACH

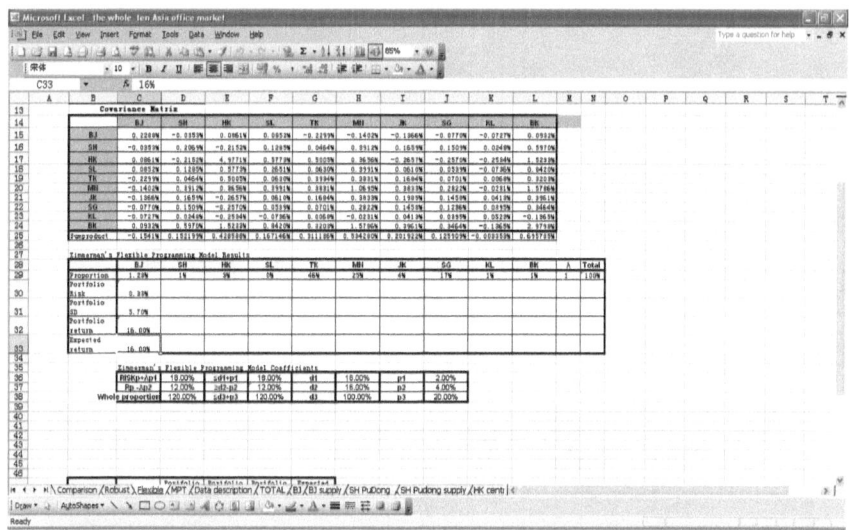

Zimmerman's FTAA flexible programming model results

	BJ	SH	HK	SL	TK	MN	JK	SG	KL	BK	λ	Total
Proportion	1.28%	1%	3%	0%	46%	25%	4%	17%	1%	1%	1	100%
Portfolio Risk	0.33%											
Portfolio SD	5.70%											
Portfolio return	16.00%											
Expected return	16.00%											

Source: Author (2020).

2. The Ramik and Rimanek FTAA robust programming model coefficients

mx	14.48%	P	14.50%	εl	0.00%	$\_\varepsilon l(\alpha x-\gamma)$	0.00%	$\leq p-mx$	0.02%
nx	16.48%	Q	17.50%	δl	2.00%	$\_\delta l(\alpha x-\gamma)$	0.02%	$\leq p-mx$	0.02%
αx	2.00%	Γ	3.00%	εr	2.00%	$\varepsilon r(\beta x-\delta)$	-0.02%	$\leq q-nx$	1.02%
βx	2.00%	Δ	3.00%	δr	4.00%	$\delta r(\beta x-\delta)$	0.00%	$\leq q-nx$	1.02%

Source: Author (2020).

The membership function of this fuzzy TAA model

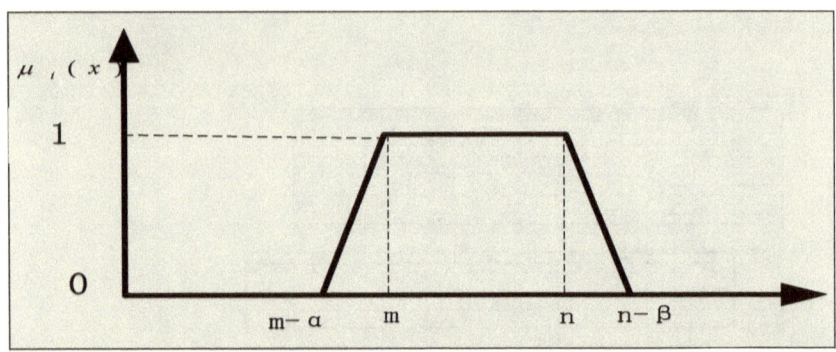

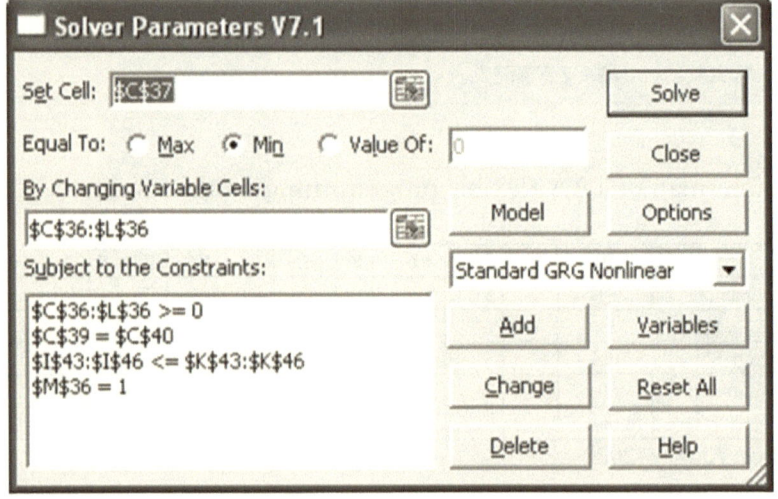

PROJECT MANAGEMENT – AN ARTIFICIAL INTELLIGENT (AI) APPROACH

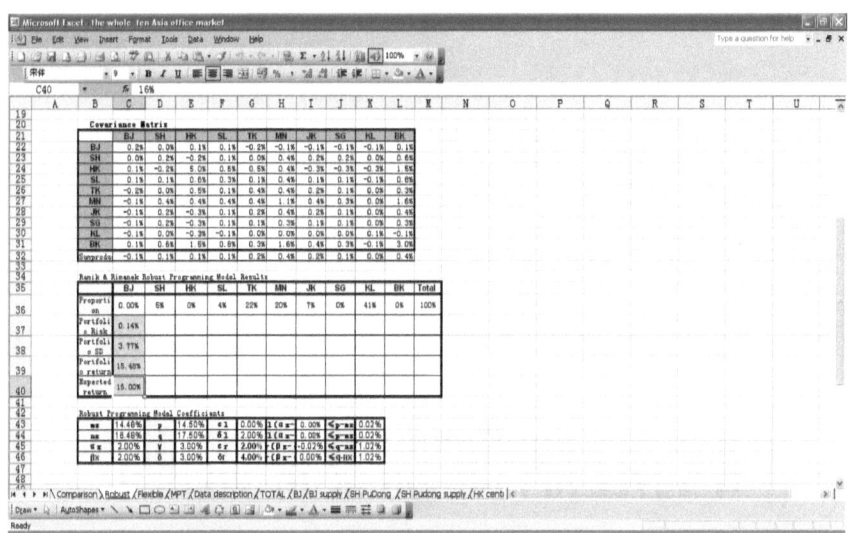

Ramik and Rimanek FTAA robust programming model results

	BJ	SH	HK	SL	TK	MN	JK	SG	KL	BK	Total
Proportion	0.00%	5%	0%	4%	22%	20%	7%	0%	41%	0%	100%
Portfolio Risk	0.14%										
Portfolio SD	3.77%										
Portfolio return	15.48%										
Expected return	16.00%										

Source: Author (2020).

CHAPTER 6

A NOVEL APPROACH OF DESIGNING THE KNOWLEDGE-BASED URBAN DEVELOPMENT (KBUD) ADOPTING THE AGENT-BASED MODEL (ABM)

Modern city planners propose localised cluster-based initiatives to stimulate innovative growth. Such initiatives are integral to sustain regional competitiveness and prosperity. Large regional and metropolitan level master plans are undertaken to develop 'knowledge-based urban developments' (KBUDs). Chapter 6 focuses on the KBUD's design via agent-based modelling. Traditional land use master planning of the mixed-use, post-industrial cluster developments are inefficient for KBUDs, subject to changing market forces. Land use objectives promote an 'interactive' physical environment, but they remain sketchy for large KBUDs. This chapter discusses the KBUD 'actors' and classifies them based on their interaction needs with other agents. A potential knowledge interaction design criteria (KIDC) is introduced with the aim of enhancing the KBUD's 'knowledge interactions' amongst different actors. The theoretical framework for a generic 'KBU-land use design model' (KBUD-LUDM) is proposed. Such a model looks at the dynamic KBUD's mixed land uses, utilising data from Singapore's public authority, the Jurong Town Corporation, for its one-north industrial real estate research park case study. The chapter discusses the KIDC that facilitates and enhances the intra-cluster interaction for post-industrial real estate developments and the dynamic KBUD-LUDM that offers an alternative flexible approach to traditional land use master planning.

The knowledge-based economy can be defined to be the major production and services centre, 'based on knowledge-intensive activities that contribute to an accelerated pace of technological and scientific advancement, and rapid obsolescence' (Powell and Snellman 2004; OECD 2000). Industrialised nations have undertaken large urban industrial real estate developments, known as the 'knowledge-based urban development' (KBUD).[1] Knight (1995) defines the transformation of knowledge resources into local development that can provide a basis for sustainable development. From an economic viewpoint, the KBUD can be defined as 'one in which economic growth is centred on the production, distribution and use of technology' (Bajracharya and Too 2009). A more planning-oriented definition is that KBUDs are a cluster of research and development (R & D) activities, high-tech manufacturing of knowledge-intensive industrial and business sectors that are linked by the mixed-use environment comprising housing, business, education, and leisure within an urban-like setting (Yigitcanlar et al. 2008). The planning-oriented definition views the KBUD as a new planning paradigm in the knowledge-based society, in which the 'ultimate goal is for a city to be designed to encourage and enable the production and circulation of abstract work' (Cheng et al. 2004). Combined with globally oriented consultancies and services, the resultant network helps to disseminate new knowledge between different actors (Gadrey et al. 1995; Hertog 2000; Muller and Zenker 2001a).

At the broader urban policy level to facilitate the KBUDs, the major goal is to adopt the 'triple helix model' of innovation by Etzkowitz and Leydesdorff (2000). Their model hypothesises the interaction amongst three key institutions: government, university, and private sector. Actors in the key institutions comprise the high-technology firms; public, private, and university research institutions; the polytechnics, the schools, and the supporting knowledge intensive business services (KIBS) that help to bring about the 'system of innovation'.[2] The availability of a diversity of resources to learn enables technology firms to better innovate. These firms interact with other firms and with other participants in the cluster like the universities, research institutes, suppliers, and consumers. The outcome is 'interactive learning' (Lundvall 1985). Several studies have documented rising improvements in the firms' innovative capability when firms interact with their participating actors (Cooke 2001; Coombs et al. 1996; Freeman and Soete 1997; Oerlemans et al. 2001; Pavitt et al. 1987; Von Hippel 1976). Urban planning studies accorded due interest in post-industrial cluster development under the KBUD paradigm (Carrillo 2004; Yigitcanlar, Velibeyoglu, and Martinez-Fernandez 2008). Earlier KBUD studies advocate the social, institutional, and cultural aspects that are imperative for the sustainable growth of planned clusters (Isaksen 2004; Knight 1995; Yigitcanlar 2009). The literature has identified five broad themes that most knowledge-based developments strive to achieve the following (Yigitcanlar et al. 2008):

- living and working,
- centrality,
- connectivity,
- learning and playing, and
- branding.

The living and working theme for mixed-use developments denotes a central goal of the KBUD, like the Helsinki Digital Village in Finland and the Kelvin Grove Urban Village in Brisbane; while the learning and playing theme is an inherent part of the KBUD, like the Copenhagen Crossroads and the Zaragoza Digital Mile in Spain. Connectivity to a global talent pool and the intra-cluster physical connectivity through pedestrian-oriented urban design denote the central goals of Singapore's one-north industrial real estate research park development. The city branding or rebranding theme creates new symbolic value to old industrial cities (Bajracharya and Too 2009). Such a theme includes the knowledge-based developments like the Taipei 101, the @22 Barcelona, and the Seoul Digital Media City.

According to Searle and Pritchard (2008), the KBUDs can be divided into three types of clusters, based on what activity type they support. The first activity type includes the knowledge-intensive service cluster that houses corporate headquarters and the higher order business and financial services—that is, the 'Financial City' model. The second activity type clusters specialised high technology research and development (R & D) activities in fields like information and communications technology (ICT), the life sciences (biomedical and biotechnology), and the media industries (e.g., Singapore's Biopolis industrial real estate research park, Maryland's DNA valley, and Cambridge's Science Park). The third activity type hosts creative fields for cultural knowledge production like the arts, media, and entertainment industries (e.g., Seoul's Digital Media City, Media City UK, 22@Barcelona, and Gold Coast Cultural and Civic Precinct and Brisbane Kelvin Grove Urban Village).

The literature focuses on case studies to evaluate the institutional and governance aspects (Chatzkel 2004; Garcia 2004; Isaksen 2004; Knight 1995; Yigitcanlar 2009; Yigitcanlar et al. 2012; Yigitcanlar et al. 2008). The literature is concerned with the development of institutional planning models and the identification of metrics that evaluate the performance of the knowledge-based developments. Various authors look at the generalised institutional planning model approaches, which the planning authorities can adopt to create sustainable developments. Such model approaches include the KBUD analysis model (Yigitcanlar 2008), the KBUD characteristics model (Van Winden et al. 2007), the KnowCis model (Ergazakis et al.

2006), the Alert model (Corey and Wilson 2006), and the famous MAKC$_i$ model established by the World Capital Institute in 2006. There has been limited studies that look at effective urban design strategies.

Two gaps in the KBUD literature are worth exploring. First, few people[3] looked at the functional role possibility that physical design can play to induce or facilitate intra-cluster interactions of the KBUD real estate. Such intra-cluster interactions enable a vibrant and interactive local environment, a phenomenon known as the 'local buzz' (Asheim et al. 2007; Bathelt et al. 2004). Urban design is an important medium to bring the related actors closer on the ground for mutual benefit. Mixed-use zoning policies stipulate adjacent and overlapping land uses to separate compatible and incompatible land uses in cities via complementary zoning. Urban design strategies for knowledge-based clusters remain highly experimental. They tend to look at the aesthetic attributes to create iconic and futuristic architectural landscapes.[4] The land use design role of facilitating spontaneous and planned interactions for knowledge-based clusters remains a major avenue that is less explored in the literature.

Second, the static designs of long-term master plans are becoming an unfavourable option for the dynamic design of the KBUDs, wherein the inflow and outflow of people and businesses imply that the KBUD urban planning and design should take them into consideration. Long-term predetermined 'zoning' plans, often a product of the underlying KBUD urban design, do not materialise on the ground, owing to ever-changing market conditions (Abukhater 2009; Torres 2006). Urban design has been depicted to be a 'black box' in the urban development process, owing to the presence of subjective and often conflicting design goals of the planners and designers (Schlager 1965). As a result, two questions can be posed:

- What is an optimal urban design criteria[5] for the KBUD that can potentially enhance intra-cluster knowledge interactions?

- How can the KBUD be dynamically[4] designed as the specialised large industrial real estate?

These questions pose important implications for urban planners and designers of knowledge-based clusters for creating vibrant mixed-use specialised large industrial real estate. Hence, chapter 6 comprises several sections, with the first section providing the introduction. The next (second) section is concerned with the related literature on the KBUD's knowledge-based interactions of high-technology clusters, inclusive of its associated actors, on innovation and proximity dynamics. The third section looks at the knowledge interaction design criteria (KIDC), which, in turn, provides the KBUD land use design guidelines. The fourth section discusses chapter 6's approach, the drawbacks of land use design models (LUDMs); the conceptual framework of the KBUD-land use design model (KBUD-LUDM) that adopts the agent-based large industrial real estate model approach; the model's data requirements; and the model itself as a meaningful KBUD design tool. The fifth section concludes the chapter.

The Related Literature

The importance of knowledge in catalysing the process of technological innovation is reiterated in the science and technology literature (Hargadon and Sutton 1997; Kanter 1988; Mascitelli 2000; Nonaka and Konno 1998). Individuals working in knowledge-intensive industries require information resources within their spatial horizon to facilitate the consumption of existing information. Face-to-face interaction amongst the individual workers is an important medium that facilitates the creation, sharing, and transfer of knowledge. Such interaction denotes the consultations amongst peers that involve the task-related exchange of information. Sonnenwald (1999) has shown that workers, exposed to a large

---

[4] or incrementally.

number of information resources (like the mentors, the peers for consultation, the literature, and the subject experts) would expand their knowledge more than the unexposed groups of workers. Earlier studies highlight the important face-to-face consultation of the knowledge-related workspaces. In his seminal analysis on R & D projects, Allen (1984) showed that an increase in the number of consultations amongst research groups would correlate with higher subjective expert ratings of R & D effectiveness. In studying team performance of an education department, Ancona and Caldwell (1992) find that knowledge expansion would accrue from face-to-face worker interaction that benefit overall team performance. Salter and Gann (2003) demonstrated that the non-routine patterns of work[6] of high-technology workers are dependent on the face-to-face peer interaction for problem solving and ideas transfer. Such studies provide a strong basis for enabling the design community to support the notion that there exists a potential contribution for work place planning, which essentially moulds human behaviour and interactions in the R & D oriented environments (Toker and Gray 2008).

Design studies advocate the design of workspace that emphasises the provision of informal spaces and social amenities, like the cafes, bars, and restaurants that promote social interactions. Coupled with private spaces to support concentrated work enables the formation of the creative environment via readily facilitating information exchange (Duffy 1997; Duffy et al. 2012). Studies on the beneficial effects of design to sustain face-to-face interactions are limited for the micro environment (e.g., at the real estate asset level). There appears to be a lack of understanding with regard to how design can benefit the large-scale knowledge-based developments. For the planned knowledge-based clusters, the influence of spatial design does not exist at the real estate asset level but beyond that, at the urban precinct[7] level. Land use design becomes important that helps to shape the relative position of the workers in space. Once the land use design characteristics of the participating actors and the determinants of their interaction amongst the actors are understood, such information can be utilised to create efficient land use designs for KBUDs. By placing the related actors together, complementary land use designs can be created, and they support the interaction patterns of peers within and across the scientific fields.

Urban design makes the connections between people, places, movement, and urban form.[8] Urban design is conducted by zoning instruments, stipulating that adjacent or overlapping land uses are identified and separated into compatible and incompatible land uses in urban spaces. The urban designer's role is to identify the types of connections or interactions[9] amongst the actors and their determinants to enable various land uses to be arranged in space. When formulating design goals for the large KBUD, it is useful to rely on some basic principles of formulating the design criteria by Lynch and Rodwin (1958). They recognise that the goal formulation process for any city or large real estate development project should enhance two important relationships in space:

- the relationship of men and objects that relate people and buildings in their functional role;
- the relationship of men and men that is concerned with an interpersonal relation, like that for constructing surroundings that maximise interpersonal communications.

The first relationship is concerned with generating functional goals with regard to the type of environment that is to be achieved by the design—for example, a historical town, a housing neighbourhood, or an industrial real estate development. Lynch and Rodwin (1958) reiterate that first relationship denotes the sensual interactions between men and objects (i.e., the industrial real estate assets). Such interactions include aesthetical and physiological goals, which are to be achieved by the design—for example, the Victorian architectural facades for old town renewal programmes or the futuristic designs of modern industrial real estate developments.

The second relationship is concerned with the explicit need to understand the relationship amongst individuals belonging to the different functional buildings or economic activities. This relationship can be a simple spatial connection like the relationship between housing and schools or retail shopping, between business activity and the transportation corridor. This spatial connection can influence how people interact with each other, how they move around, and how they use a place for different purposes.[10] This second relationship is more relevant for designing interactive spaces and achieving efficient land use design.

The KBUD interactions are of a higher order. Land use design facilitates the interaction between related workers that exist through collaboration, say, between the scientists of one organisation (e.g., a high technology software firm) with another (e.g., a university department). Therefore, the KBUD's design needs to satisfy an important design objective to create a spatial distribution, wherein the nearby actors are more likely to interact and to benefit from positive externalities. There is very little guidance for urban planners and designers to be cognisant of the nature of the participating actors, their characteristics in terms of the type of work they are involved in, and their interaction patterns with one another. Chapter 6 seeks to fill this shortcoming.

First, the definition and the nature of the KBUD knowledge interactions are explored, to be followed by a short account of the participating actors together with their characteristics in terms of the types of work they perform. Second, four determinants of the knowledge interaction amongst knowledge-based workers are identified from the innovation and proximity dynamics literature. Third, the design criteria is proposed that house actors in space to achieve maximum interaction. Departing from the linear programming approach that has dominated previous land use design models, an agent-based model approach is adopted to facilitate the KBUD design process (Barber 1976; Correia and Madden 1985; Janssen van Herwijnen, Stewart, and Aerts 2008; Schlager 1965; Williams, ReVelle, and Levin 2004).

Knowledge interactions (KIs) denote 'the continuous and dynamic interaction(s) between tacit and explicit knowledge that occur at the individual, group, organizational and inter-organizational levels, which lead to the creation or sharing or the transfer of knowledge and information' (Nonaka and Takeuchi 1995). Recent studies on knowledge-based clusters identify the various types and channels through which interactions occur amongst the actors involved in the innovation process. KIs can occur through interpersonal relationships (i.e., personal, professional, and mixed ones) that are formed as a result of intra-cluster collaborations (e.g., in contract research); human capital transfers (i.e., intra-cluster job transfers); major events (e.g., conferences and trade fairs); field- and sector-based communities (e.g., research-based consortiums) via the sharing of capital resources (e.g., public and private grants and expensive equipment); and the unplanned accidental encounters (Asheim et al. 2007; Kesidou, Caniëls, and Romijn 2009; Lawson and Lorenz 1999; Meeus et al. 2004). Spatial proximity plays an important role to support knowledge interactions (KIs) through the formation of interpersonal relationships (formal and informal ones) and planned or unplanned encounters. According to Foray (2005), barriers to the interaction amongst the 'related actors'[11] are most sensitive to the expansion of geographical distance.

Utilising spatial and behavioural data collected from knowledge-based companies, Rashid et al. (2006) showed that spatial layouts consistently influence worker movements and their subsequent interactions. At the building level, spatial layout is important in facilitating 'useful' KIs. Some studies provide empirical evidence to show that the rising mean integration of an area of a building would increase integration amongst the workers, as evidenced by rising interactions' frequency (Hillier et al. 1990; Penn and Hillier 1992). By providing adequate amenities, opportunities can be created for knowledge workers to meet and interact. When such land use deigns bring complementary or interdependent knowledge activities together through mixed-use zoning, then the overall probability of useful interactions improves. As the related actors are brought close to one another through mixed-use zoning strategies, the actors and workers readily benefit from positive externalities through planned and spontaneous 'face-to-face' interactions. There is limited discussion in the literature on classifying the 'actors' in terms of their KIs and their relation(s) to space. Different types of actors interact, share, and transfer knowledge in different ways. For example, an engineer may require frequent interactions with his supervisor, as the engineer's job entails more of the 'learning by doing' in comparison to a biotechnologist, who acquires new knowledge through codified information, such as from journal articles and news. The intuitive way to achieve high levels of interactions in land use design would be to mix a variety of uses and to simultaneously step up the overall density of the industrial real estate development. The average spatial proximity amongst the participants on-site is reduced accordingly. For the KIs to occur between any two agents (or two workers), the spatial proximity is just one factor amongst others (Boschma 2005). Therefore, there is the need to classify the KBUD actors.

Table 6.1 presents the KBUD classification of its actors. The classification defines the actors concerned and each actor's role specific to the KBUD. Every actor not only performs a unique function but also reflects a possible interaction with one another. The first actor—for example, the university—acts as the locus of knowledge generation in knowledge-based clusters because universities are deemed to be the sources of new knowledge (Anselin et al. 1997; Feldman 1994; Saxenian 1994). Knowledge diffusion from university research can occur through formal cooperation with firms via the mobility of university graduates into firms; and via informal social interactions between employees and university researchers (Torre and Rallet 2005; Vas 2009). Studies find a significant and positive effect of the presence of universities in locations with higher start-up rates; R & D facilities; high-technology production, and human capital (Bania, Calkins, and Dalenberg 1992; De Meyer 1991; Nelson 1986; Rees and Stafford 1986). Anselin et al. (1997) reiterate the importance of university research, owing to 'the importance of basic university research in the stimulation of technological innovation and higher productivity that is derived from the public good nature of the research, and the resulting positive externalities to the private sector in the form of knowledge spillovers'.

Public research institutes' (PRI) role in the innovation process is well documented, deploying case studies that concentrate on the analysis of high-technology clusters like Silicon Valley in the Austin and San Antonio Corridor, Route 128 in Boston, the Cambridge Science Park region, and the Phoenix area in the UK (Hobday 1988; Saxenian 1996; Segal, Smilor, Kozmetsky, and Gibson 1988; Smilor et al. 1987; Wigand 1988). PRIs have several channels of achieving their role. PRIs are engaged in the codification of information, in the publishing of scientific materials in journals, in undertaking contract research with firms in the form of joint R & D projects, in providing consulting programs to organisations, and in the training of personnel from industry (Fritsch and Schwirten 1999; Cooke 2001; Cooke, Uranga, and Etxebarria 1998). Face-to-face interactions are highlighted to be important channels of knowledge transfer, and that the geographic proximity of PRIs and the private sector forms the crucial component of the regional innovation systems (RIS). PRIs like the Brookings, Scripps, and Carnegie Mellon institutes, the extra university research arms like the Max Plank and Rockefeller institutes, non-governmental organisations (NGOs) like the WRI, Greenpeace, and the Amnesty International NGOs[5] can create a group of actors that are involved in the innovation process through applied research. Most NGOs conduct research that addresses socially pressing issues—for example, AIDS, tuberculosis, and dengue fever. They often conduct experimental research programs. Technology firms denote the locus of industrial production and central agents for commercialising and distributing new technology, innovation, and output associated with firm entry; networks and higher productivity growth (Acs and Audretsch 1990; Elfring and Hulsink 2003; Smith et al. 2005). Knowledge transfer amongst firms in the cluster that have strong manufacturing and R & D core can readily benefit from the inherent geographic proximity (Baptista and Swann 1998; Pavitt 1987).

---

[5] WRI, World Resources Institute.

Table 6.1. Classification of participants of the knowledge-based urban development (KBUD) by their role in the knowledge-based economy

Participants	Role in the knowledge cluster
University	Primary driver of knowledge creation
Public Research Institute (PRI)	State-funded basic and applied research (civilian- and defence-related)
Private, extra-university research institutes, NGO research establishments	Promotes more niche, goal-oriented, socially pressing research programs, clinical trial-oriented experimental research programs
Technology firms	Commercialising innovation and product formation
Service companies (KIBS)	Often dubbed as the 'third pillar of the knowledge economy— talent agencies, IT, legal, finance (includes venture capitalists), real estate services, etc.

Source: Author (2020).

The services sector plays a direct role in the innovation process and is known as the knowledge-intensive business services (KIBS). Services firms denote those 'firms (that perform) mainly for other firms, encompassing highly (intellectual) and value (adding) services' (Muller and Zenker 2001b). Such services firms are of two types:

- traditional knowledge-intensive business services (KIBS); and
- new technology, knowledge-intensive business services (NKIBS).

The services sector is referred to as the third pillar of the knowledge economy that support traditional services like the IT, financial, legal, training, networking, building, and the real estate services to primarily cater to the universities, the PRIs, and the high-technology companies. Examples of new technology, knowledge-intensive business services (KIBS) include the telecommunication services, new technology training, new technologies design inclusive of precision engineering, technical engineering, and R & D consultancy services (den Hertog 2002; Hertog 2000).

Industrial clustering is ordered on three spatial scales to achieve agglomeration economies (Marshall 1920). Such clustering occurs at the regional, metropolitan, and neighbourhood levels.[12] The geographic agglomeration of economic activities is strengthened, owing to falling transportation costs in moving goods, people, and ideas. Studies have dealt with the beneficial effects of spatial proximity that enhance the processes of interactive learning and innovation. Spatial proximity facilitates trustful relationships, easy observations, and immediate comparison through face-to-face interactions (Malmberg and Maskell 2006). The KBUD localises learning through reducing the cost or barrier of transferring ideas and information via knowledge interactions (KIs). Table 6.1's KIs are concerned with face-to-face communication amongst members of the 'innovation milieu' that denotes the knowledge-based workers from the state, academia, and the private sector. The importance of KIs to facilitate innovation is well documented in the innovative milieu and in the knowledge spillover literature (Bottazzi and Peri 2003; Camagni 1991).

Generally, any actor[13] that is involved in the interactive learning process is attributable to three types of knowledge bases—that is, the analytical, synthetic, and symbolic knowledge bases. Knowledge workers who derive their expertise from the analytical knowledge base are involved in pure scientific discovery to explore the 'natural world' (Asheim et al. 2007; Moodysso et al. 2008). Knowledge workers who derive their expertise from the synthetic knowledge base are involved in the design or construction of a product to attain a specific functional goal (Moodysson et al. 2008). Actors belonging to the analytical and synthetic knowledge bases are engaged with their KIs, in comparison to the 'information interactions'.[14] Figure 6.1 depicts the classification of KIs of the knowledge-based cluster.

Fig. 6.1. Representation of interactive learning in the knowledge-based urban development (KBUD) according to their knowledge bases

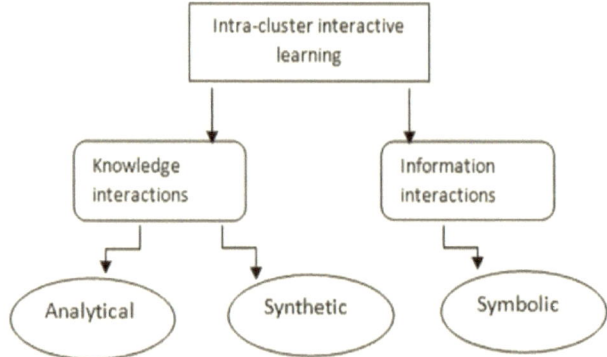

Source: Adapted from the classification by Asheim and Geltner (2005); author (2020).

Information interactions are similar to the KIs, but the information interactions are confined to those interactions that occur amongst workers from industries, who derive their expertise from the symbolic knowledge base. Examples of professions that belong to the symbolic knowledge base include those in the architecture, arts and craft, television, radio, advertising, publishing, performing arts, gaming, design, fashion, film, and music industries. Such creative industries rely on skills acquired through 'learning by doing' in formal and informal settings. It is owing to their unique work nature, where the industrial real estate development projects require constant interaction on the basis of formal and informal communication 'along the way' (Asheim et al. 2007). The simplest way to enhance interaction levels through the urban design of a KBUD is to zone all the actors according to the knowledge base, to which each actor belongs. This KBUD design type is depicted in figure 6.2, which divides the KBUD site into specialised knowledge quadrants.

Fig. 6.2. A hypothetical example of the knowledge-based urban development (KBUD) land use design deploying knowledge bases as the only design criteria

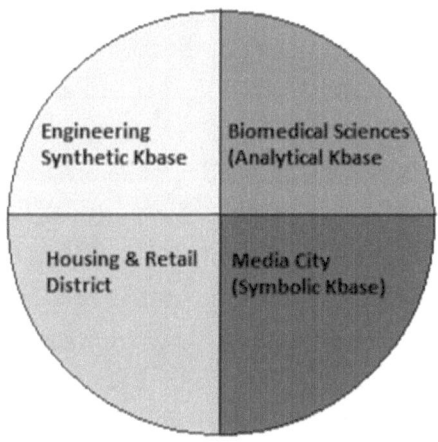

Source: Author (2020).

An appropriate example of this KBUD type, which divides its KBUD site into specialised knowledge quadrants, is Singapore's one-north industrial real estate research park, comprising knowledge specific zones for a biomedical hub like the Biopolis. The Biopolis has a large engineering complex, large sciences complex (i.e., the Fusionopolis), and large media and arts district (i.e., the Mediapolis). The notion that geographic proximity is one of the most important criteria that fosters interactive learning amongst the knowledge workers has been debunked by several authors (Asheim et al. 2007; Boschma 2005; Shaw and Gilly 2000). Co-locating[15] a diverse set of the actors concerned at the local or regional level is necessary, but that it is not a sufficient condition to stimulate 'knowledge interactions' (KIs).

Boschma (2005) alludes proximity dynamics, which are required by the actors of the innovation process, to include the institutional, cognitive, social, organisational, and geographical proximity aspects. He argues there is not just one but a confluence of all these proximity aspects that determine the probability of knowledge interactions (KIs) between any two agents or workers in space. Knowledge is often dispersed amongst the actors concerned, who, in turn, belong to different organisations. Actors in the knowledge economy denote the economic agents, who are subjected to bounded rationality.[16] The cognitive base is deemed to be any group that belongs to a particular field of science or an economic sector. Biomedical sciences have their associated economic sector to include the biomedical-related technology firms. Knowledge transfer from one agent to another often requires the interacting agents to possess an absorptive capacity to identify, interpret, and exploit new knowledge (Cohen and Levinthal 1990). Cognitive differences amongst the actors concerned can constraint one another's absorptive capacity (Simon 1955). Knowledge workers that belong to similar fields of science or similar economic sectors readily learn from one another because of their common domain expertise. Too much cognitive proximity can be detrimental to learning and innovation (Boschma 2005; Pouder and St. John 1996). Proximity amongst the actors that belong to similar cognitive bases may not be favourable to the innovation process because of three reasons.

First, the knowledge building process itself requires dissimilar and complementary bodies of knowledge to trigger new ideas and creativity. Second, too much cognitive proximity leads to the cognitive lock-in that denotes those routines within similar work-related networks, which can restrict new technologies or market opportunities. Such a lock-in leads to what is known as the 'competency trap' (Levitt and March 1988). Third, too much cognitive proximity increases the risk of involuntary knowledge spillovers, which prompt the competitors to be unwilling to share knowledge. Cantwell and Santangelo (2003) reiterate that the competing firms, who belong to similar scientific fields or economic sectors, do not co-locate their research activities to reduce the unintended spillovers.

Organisational practices are imperative to enable interactive learning (Boschma 2005). Actors within similar organisations (be they small firms, large firms, academic departments, and the polytechnics) are envisaged to share the reference and knowledge space that is bounded by an economic or a financial dependency. Such a proximity type can be divided into the intra-organisational proximity, which refers to the internal management hierarchy (be it vertical or horizontal); and into the inter-organisational proximity, which refers to the distance between two workers who belong to a similar organisation. Similar organisational arrangements act like vehicles that enable knowledge and information exchange amongst the related agents (Cooke et al. 1998).

Organisational proximity[17] amongst the actors concerned is important to enable learning and innovation. Organisational proximity asserts strong control over new knowledge creation and ownership rights that also reward its new technology efforts. Excessive proximity or too little proximity amongst the actors that belong to similar organisations can be a deterrent to learning and innovation. When there is too much inter-organisational proximity, the actors concerned are exposed to the risk of being accustomed to established relationships. As the search for novelty often requires the actors concerned to proceed out of their established networks, then too much proximity may act as a barrier (Boschma 2005).

Fig. 6.3. A hypothetical example of the knowledge-based urban development (KBUD) land use design deploying the type of organisation as the only design criteria

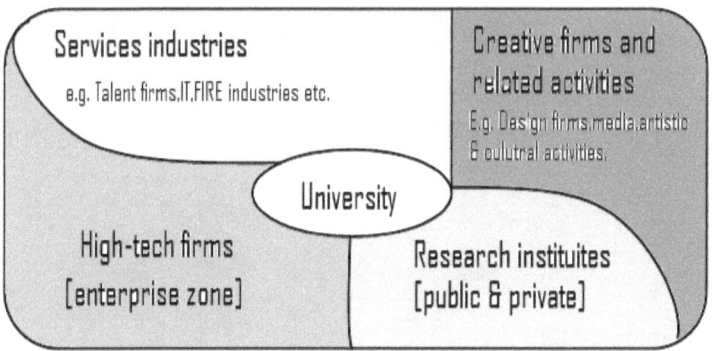

Source: Author (2020).

Too little inter-organisational proximity raises concerns of opportunism, owing to the lack of control over intellectual property and the weakening of networking capabilities amongst the agents belonging to similar organisations. Figure 6.3 depicts the hypothetical design of a KBUD that is divided along the lines of the organisational type of participants (Sarimin and Yigitcanlar 2011). The closest example of this type of urban design is the Cooroy Lower Mill KBUD in Queensland, Australia; the La Technopole de l'Aube in France; and the Cyberjaya multimedia corridor in Selangor, Malaysia. Institutional proximity refers to the proximity that is associated at the macro level of any organisational unit. For example, the public research institutions versus the private institutions share similar values and norms (North 1990). Such values and norms denote the comfort level within institutions that are characterised by 'a set of common habits, routines, established practices, rule or laws that regulate the relationships between individuals and groups' (Edquist and Johnson 1997). Inasmuch as institutional proximity can be an enabler of interactive learning amongst the workers concerned, then too much institutional proximity can constrain the knowledge interactions (Boschma 2005).

Fig. 6.4. A hypothetical example of the knowledge-based urban development (KBUD) land use design deploying the type of institution as the only design criteria

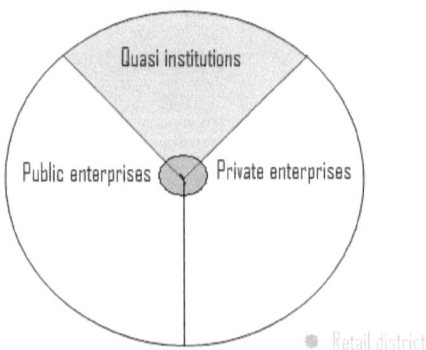

Source: Author (2020).

A well-accepted notion is that institutional environments can act as complementarities to denote the complex web of relationships amongst the various departments concerned. The result should pave the way for the institutional lock-in that would resist immediate changes (Hannan and Freeman 1977). Such inward looking hinders the development of innovation, causing institutional rigidity and leaving no room for the experimentation of new ideas. Figure 6.4 depicts the KBUD that is planned strictly on institutional zoning lines and so should reduce the mean integration of the constituent actors that belong to different institutions. Geographical or spatial proximity is defined to be that physical distance between economic actors and is the most important factor, which, in conjunction with other proximity factors, can substantially enhance the information needs for an interactive land use design of the KBUD. Studies reiterate that short distances would favour information exchange through planned or unplanned contacts and through face-to-face interactions (Audretsch and Feldman 1996; Jaffe, Trajtenberg, and Henderson 1993; Van Oort 2002). The temporary and permanent geographical clustering is found to be beneficial, with the 'short distances literally (bringing) people together, (favouring) information contact and (facilitating) the exchange of tacit knowledge. The larger the distance between the agents, the less the intensity of these positive externalities, and the more difficult it becomes to transfer tacit knowledge' (Boschma 2005).

An urban design that creates geographical proximity between the related agents can help to initiate face-to-face interaction. Increasing distance between the related knowledge workers, caused by land use designs, can dissociate related activities in space, thereby reducing the intensity of positive externalities. Let us assume a finite system represented by a two-dimensional continuous space grid S. Agents $x_1, x_2 .. x_n \in X$ represent the number of actors that are planned in the knowledge-based development. Each agent belongs to a specific type of actor (see table 1)—for example, a technology firm or a research institution. Similarly, every agent (x_i) can be classified into their constituent properties—that is, $i \in \{p,q,r,s\}$, where p holds the information on the type of knowledge base; q, the institutional base; r, the organisational base; and s, its cognitive base. Therefore,

$$x\{i\} = Agent_{\{p,q,r,s\}} \qquad (1)$$

Each agent that enters the system is to be embedded with the above and the given composite parameter for identification purposes. Full information is assumed and not new. It is easily obtainable from planning documents. For example, if a KBUD is being planned for five hundred biomedical private firms (the private label), then five hundred agents can be immediately classified to have the following characteristics: analytical (knowledge base), biomedical sciences (cognitive field), high-technology firms (organisational), and private affiliation (institutional).

As agents enter the system S, they are allocated a discrete location provided by the random coordinates (x,y). To place the agents in space to maximise knowledge interactions, geographic proximity between agents can be represented as an inverse function of their given proximity factors in that the more the proximity factors between any two agents (i,j) that share the same system, the less the distance between them in space:

$$x(Agent_{ij}) \propto \frac{1}{D_{ij}}$$

, where x represents a normalised value that is attached to each proximity factor. Equation (6.2) simply states that as the proximity factors shared between two agents (i & j) tend to be high—that is, as $x \rightarrow 1$—then the (spatial) distance between agents that belong to the same institution type approaches zero (i.e. $D_{ij} \rightarrow 0$). To prevent the lock-in phenomenon discussed earlier, the extreme case should be avoided. The land use design criteria should be able to strike a balance in determining the geographical distance between agents that share similar characteristics.

Urban design that induces greater KI levels amongst participating agents in the knowledge-based development should follow figure 6.5's nonlinear curve. From interactive learning and proximity dynamics, an urban design's interaction level with regard to each proximity factor increases up to a threshold, after which it decreases steadily. The '0' on the x-axis of figure 6.5 exhibits a design scenario that offers a minimum level of interaction, owing to the low levels of proximity amongst actors of the urban design. The '1' corresponds to a maximum level of proximity, showing the same low levels of interaction. An optimal design approach would be to mix the planned KBUD participants to produce a satisfactory mix of all proximity factors, represented by the shaded region, ω, in figure 6.5.

Fig. 6.5. Theoretical urban design criteria for a knowledge interactive environment, ω

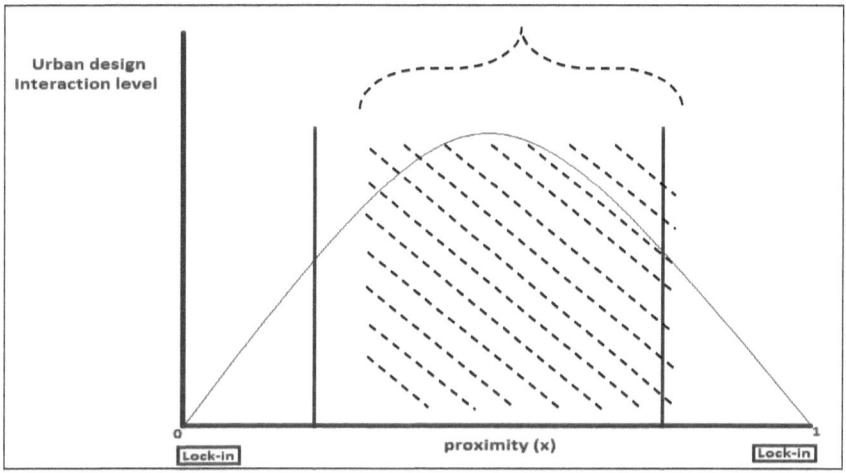

Source: Author (2020).

The urban design outcome depends on the planner's decision as to which basis he wants to mix the land uses. For example, if the planner only aims for complete institutional proximity—that is, $I(x \rightarrow 1)$—between agents in the design, then the KBUD permits agents of the same institutions to co-locate.[6] To maximise the knowledge and information interactions, the aim is to create an urban design that positions the most related actors (i.e., actors related on more than one proximity dimension would be close to each other). Summarising and to attain an optimal land use design, the spatial position of all

---

[6] See figure 6.

agents in the system must be governed by a minimisation function, which minimises the mean linear distance between any two agents that are related by one or more levels of proximity. Thus, the agents that are more closely related are placed together, as opposed to agents that do not share any similarity in their type of scientific or economic field, their organisation or institution. Few inferences can be made from chapter 6's foregoing theoretical framework. A land use plan designed only on institutional lines should create physical barriers to the cross-fertilisation of ideas across the actors belonging to different institutions. It does not mean that such interactions would not occur but safe to say that the physical design may not be able to reinforce existing connections, in space between related activities. To show the inherent complexity of the physical design process, a formal model can be proposed that includes not only the design criteria but also other facets of the design process.

The Approach

Traditionally, urban planning, design and development master plans normally include projections of population growth, the allocation of specific activities across space (i.e., the design), and that the corresponding demand for future services would altogether inform the adequate zoning of land parcels. Nineteenth-century planning ideas were useful when the projection growth rates were slow and predictable, but such planning ideas pose a challenge to planners, who today encounter dynamic and unpredictable projection growth rates. The situation is true for a complex industrial real estate development. The KBUD accommodates a variety of activities, and it is in a constant state of change, owing to economic uncertainty. In this time and age, it is not an exaggeration to state that long-term master plans and urban designs end up on the bookshelves and in the closets of real estate developers, because these plans and designs are hardly used as a guide to inform the future path of design and urban development (Torres 2006). As a result, planned real estate developments lose their design goals because the static urban development plans are incompatible with the KBUD's dynamically changing complex system.

Cities are complex systems based on their characteristics of self-similarity, self-organisation, and on the emergence of patterns, which can be exhibited by the non-linear behaviour of land use demand over time (Batty and Longley 1994). KBUDs are large self-sustaining enclaves with as many land uses as a city itself, and with some KBUDs scaling up to as big as mini cities (e.g., Seoul's Digital Media City KBUD).

There are many advantages in adopting agent-based modelling (ABM) over simple linear systems and applying the resultant models to develop planning tools that help to plan complex systems. ABM helps to gain knowledge about the dynamics of the land use design process. Modelling is often conducted in conjunction with an integrated geographic information system (GIS) (the spatial dimension) and with temporal dynamics (the time dimension), all of which arise from agent-agent and agent-environment interactions (Torres 2006). Earlier land use design models that adopt the single and multiple equation systems are found to lack the meaningful feedback mechanism, supported by the dynamic ABM.

According to Schlager (1965), the land use design model (LUDM) is a conscious synthesis of urban form to meet human needs. The KBUD has the need to maximise interaction via minimising the space between related actors, who may engage in useful interactions on a frequent basis. Earlier LUDMs adopt linear programming techniques to generate optimal urban designs for a set of design goals under certain capacity constraints. Examples include LUDMs by Schlager (1965), Barber (1976), Arad and Berechman (1978), Williams et al. (2004), Makowski et al. (2000), Janssen et al. (2008), Diamond and Wright (1988), Correia and Madden (1985), and Davis and Grant (1987).

Chapter 6 proposes the ABM that has inherent advantages over the simple equation-based modelling approach in addressing spatial and temporal dynamics. ABM is a multi-agent systems model, adopted to model various social and economic problems. Well-known ABM applications find that they are not limited to the organisational behaviour field (Hughes et al. 2012), to the supply chain optimisation (Fox et al. 2000), to consumer behaviour (Said et al. 2002), to portfolio management (Niu et al. 2003), to pedestrian flow (Batty 2003), and to traffic congestion and management (Dresner and Stone 2004). Only recently, Ligtenberg et al. (2004) demonstrate the ABM use and its applicability to resolve spatial planning problems.

The LUDM attempts to plan for a set of well-defined n number of agents or state 'variables'. The agents enter the system for a given period of time either in a continuous or in a discrete manner (groups):

$$\int_0^n Agents = x_1, x_2, x_3 \ldots \ldots x_n \qquad (6.3)$$

The basic components of a LUDM can be denoted via deploying three sets of variables—namely, quality, quantity, and location. These variables constitute the overall urban design model (Schlager 1965). The quality variable represents the type of land use in demand—for example, the demand for industrial real estate research park space to host future biomedical research activity that may require high-specification industrial land uses. Full information is assumed for the type of actors and their characteristics, as expressed in equation (6.1). Their land use demand can be determined by the number and the type of actors that enter the system, as expressed in the following manner:

$$G_i = \beta_0 x_1 + \beta_2 x_2 + \beta_3 x_3 \ldots \beta_n x_n \qquad (6.4)$$

, where G_i denotes the total land use demand for the planning region.

The coefficients $x_1..n$ denote the individual demand for each type of land use (i.e., industrial high technology, residential, and office space), along with the specific constant β_x that represent the subsidiary service ratio coefficients—for example, the streets, toilets, and open space.[18] The land use type is derived from the set of agents entering the system S. The location variable is denoted by the interaction term, implying which agents are more compatible than others. Agents are enabled to share the same characteristics to co-locate in space, and from which the complementary land uses can be inferred. An optimal design criterion needs to create an equal trade-off between the four proximity factors amongst all agents in the system. Once the optimal system design criterion is imposed, the agents are subjected to the following minimisation function:

$$\overline{D}_{p,q,r,s} \operatorname*{Min}_{i=2}^{n} \sum (x_i) \tag{6.5}$$

, where the term x_i denotes a generic agent that is represented by equation (6.5). $\overline{D}_{p,q,r,s}$ is the mean linear distance between the agents that share similar characteristics p, q, r, s.

Equation (6.5) states that for all agents in the system $x_{1,2...n} \in X$, each can be represented by their characteristic parameters p, q, r, s, to minimise the mean linear distance between agents that belong to the same parameter class (i.e., p, q, r, s). The minimisation function is subjected to two spatial constraints, denoting the quantity variables of the model. Such constraints constitute the spatial constraints on land parcels or the entire planning region—for example, plot area, plot ratio, gross floor area (GFA), and population limits. The quantity variables constrain the length, breadth, and height of the industrial real estate development project. They are given either through the equation (6.3) regional population controls—that is, person per acre, (F_n) or through the upper limits on each land parcel in equation (6.4), such as the plot ratios (x_i):

$$\sum_{x_0}^{n} n_x < F_N \qquad (6.6)$$

$$x_1 + x_2 + x_3 \ldots x_n \leq F_x \qquad (6.7)$$

, where n is the total population expected of the proposed industrial real estate development and F_n is the artificial limit imposed. F_x is the upper limit that restricts the buildable height on land parcels. The alternative in planning practice is the gross floor area (GFA) ratio and/or the plot ratio (PR).

A generalised planning approach for the proposed KBUD-LUDM that adopts the ABM is depicted in the system diagram of figure 6.6. The employment and population forecasts are external to the KBUD-LUDM and are assumed to be the given inputs. They include information about the number and types of industries planned (i.e., the knowledge bases), the types of organisations that are expected to be accommodated (e.g., the technology firms, the services, and the RIs), the participating institutions (e.g., the public, private, and quasi institutions), along with their respective industrial classification of their scientific fields or economic sectors (i.e., the cognitive bases). This information set generates an approximate number and the types of agents that are expected to participate in the KBUD agent initialisation procedure (AIP). The second set of inputs constitutes geographical information on the land parcels (i.e., the coordinate map) and their corresponding constraints (e.g. plot ratios, height restrictions, and the real estate asset conservation list). The inputs set are optimised[19] to generate a spatial design that satisfies the urban design goal of maximising the knowledge interaction design criteria (KIDC). It is readily observed how other constraints may be required to generate a more comprehensive KBUD design. The literature shows that the cost constraints constitute a favourable option for the land use design optimisation problem. Compatible soil types and the transportation constraints can be considered (Diamond and Wright 1988; Opdam et al. 1965; Williams et al. 2004).

The Data

A detailed rendition of land use design as an output is crucial in achieving widespread acceptance by urban planners and public authorities (Schlager 1965). Chapter 6 outlines the required data (i.e., the input parameters) for the KBUD-LUDM to generate meaningful land use designs. Three primary data sets are required to support the numerical, computational process. Data sets include the spatial information on demarcated land parcels and location on the planned site—that is, in the computer-aided design (CAD) file format. From figure 6.6, regional economic forecasts on an approximate number of participants and their characteristics are planned for the industrial real estate development.

Additional input data include the physical constraints like the supra urban density restrictions (e.g., the plot ratios, height restrictions, and building setbacks), the gross floor area (GFA), and the government's reserved sites that are avoided—that is, lands that are unsuitable for real estate development and the conservation sites. Minimum requirements include supplementary land uses like the number of libraries, seminar halls, cafes, retail outlets, car parks, lot coverage, and green spaces. Collectively, such land uses from local or regional planning authorities enable a more comprehensive urban design.

Fig. 6.6. A system diagram of the agent-based land use design planning proces

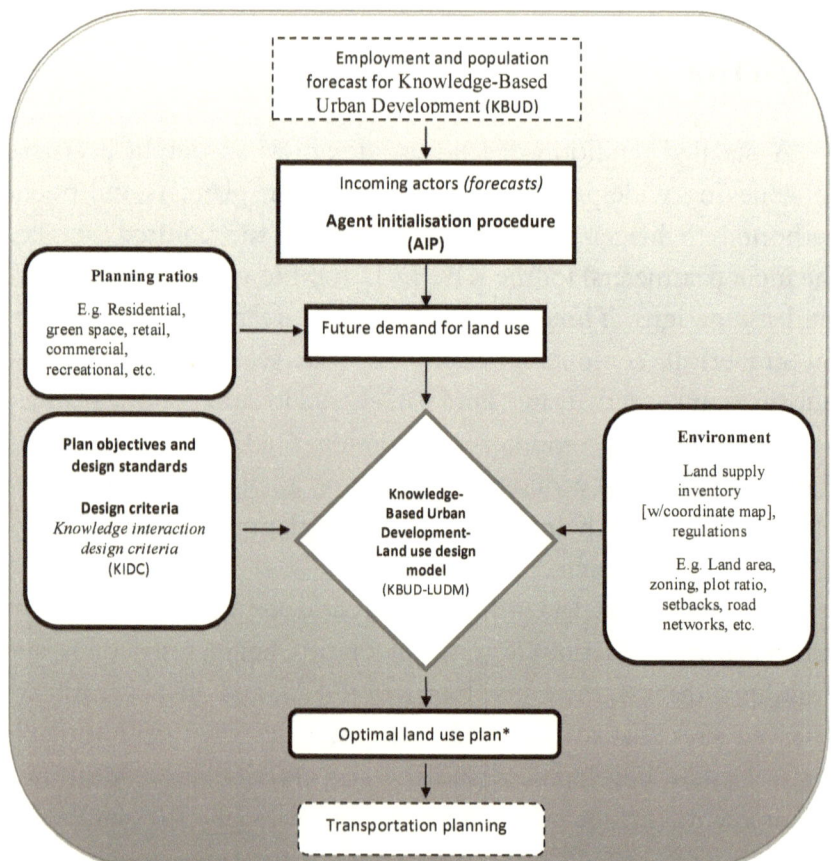

Source: Author (2020).

Results and Findings

Simulation results are concerned with the knowledge-based urban development land use design model (KBUD-LUDM) for the case study of one-north knowledge KBUD development. The simulation results look at the basic assumptions of the KBUD-LUDMs that are required to initialise and conduct the scenario analysis. Next, the baseline scenario simulation discusses the KBUD-LUDM's agent initialisation procedure (AIP), partially estimated from surveys and interviews. The baseline scenario is examined in two parts, with the first part constructing such a scenario and is deployed as a benchmark to project scenarios of plausible future states of one-north. The second part demonstrates the KBUD-LUDM's flexibility in conducting incremental planning because land use demand fluctuates over time and into the future. Due attention is extended to the validation and visualisation procedures of future states of the KBUD-LUDM at one-north. Thereafter, future directions look at the KBUD-LUDM via multiple design criteria for comprehensive multidimensional land use design modelling.

The Model Assumptions

Planning models to simulate future scenarios for the knowledge-based urban developments (KBUDs) require basic assumptions on incoming actors. Such assumptions enable planners to estimate the necessary space, to accommodate land use types, amenities, and other physical infrastructural requirements. First and foremost, it is essential to examine a general description of the classification of the agents who participate in the KBUDs; then the minimum space requirements of both agent types—namely, primary and secondary—via adopting simple planning ratio techniques.

Agent characteristics

All actors in the knowledge-based urban development (KBUD) project are classified into two major types: primary and secondary agents. Primary agents are further divided into four major types based on their organisational nature, such as

i. technology firm,
ii. research institution,
iii. educational Institution, and
iv. service firm.

Therefore, each primary agent entering the KBUD-land use design model (KBUD-LUDM) has a unique set of characteristics, which provides the heterogeneity required to represent all actor types of the KBUD project.

Figure 6.1 is a modified version representing the agent characteristics used in the one-north KBUD-LUDM. As information on the different types of cognitive base is unavailable, it may be reasonable to leave it out of the model for simplification purposes. Intuitional differentiation is limited to two (i.e., public and private), instead of the previously proposed three (i.e., private, public and quasi). The reason is that the master plans do not document any evidence of one-north hosting quasi (private-public) institutional actors. The agent characteristics of the KBUD-LUDM are specified in figure 6.1, which depicts a hypothetical declared *agent*$_i$ containing information about the knowledge base, institutional base, and organisational base as the agents enter the KBUD project through the agent initialisation procedure (AIP).

Fig. 6.1. Defining the actor/agent characteristics of the KBUD-LUDM agent-based model

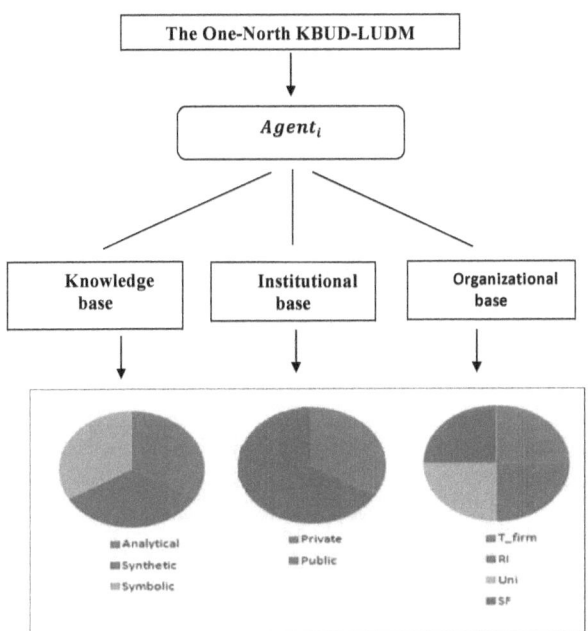

Source: Author (2020).

Space Requirements (Primary and Secondary Agents)

The agent-based land use design model for one-north is modelled on essential assumptions that are required for a holistic design approach. These are standard urban planning ratios related to space requirements that remain constant through every cycle of simulation. All agents in the system can be classified into primary agents and secondary (subsidiary) agents. The primary agents are the technology firms, like bioengineering and information technology (IT); research institutions, like basic and applied research; education, like schools, universities, and polytechnics; and service firms, like the finance, insurance, and real estate (FIRE) services, talent firms, and other networking services. Table 6.2 shows the space requirements for the primary agents according to their organisation types, which are adopted for the knowledge-based urban development-land use design model (KBUD-LUDM).

Table 6.2. Agent classification and planning parameter assumptions

Agent type	Assumptions
Technology firm	• Minimum unit of occupation: firm • Minimum number of persons/firm: 15 • Space per person: 120 sq ft • Minimum space per agent = 1,500 sq ft
Research institution	• Unit of occupation: department/NGO • Minimum number of persons/department: 10 • Space per person: 120 sq ft • Minimum space per agent = 1,200 sq ft
Educational institution (School, university etc.)	• Unit of occupation: department • Minimum number of persons/department: 10 • Space per person: 100 sq ft • Minimum space per agent = 1,200 sq ft
Miscellaneous service industries (legal, venture capitalists, talent agencies & FIRE)	• Unit of occupation: firm • Minimum number of persons/firm: 13 • Space per person: 100 sq ft • Minimum space per agent = 1,300 sq ft

Source: Author (2020).

The first required parameter for each type of agent is the *minimum unit of occupation,* stating what type of tenant entity it belongs to—that is, what is the type of the occupying agent? It can be a firm or a department. The second parameter, *minimum number of persons,* is required for each agent type—planners then get an idea of the space needed for incoming actors. Last, *space per person* is a constant usually assumed in master plans for different types of activity. The KBUD-LUDM requires minimum standards to estimate the total buildable space for each land unit. While it is true that these minimum standard parameters may not be optimal for other cities, the parameter values are validated only for the one-north case study in Singapore. Such parameter values are obtained from intensive consultations with

Singapore's Jurong Town Corporation (JTC) planners. The space per agent (SPA) value associated with every agent represents the total amount of minimum space required (in square feet) for each agent entering the KBUD project. The SPA is expressed in equation (6.1).

Space per agent (SPA)= Minimum number of persons per unit × Space per person
$$(6.1)$$

The subsidiary agents represent supporting land uses like retail and commercial real estate, recreational services, and green space requirements. In urban planning, the number of subsidiary land uses always depends on the extent of space used for primary purposes. Some examples would be the minimum space per worker, minimum bathrooms per one thousand people, and minimum space for retail and commercial space per one thousand people. It is common practice to use standard planning ratios to maintain minimum standards throughout the master plan. Such planning ratios are often derived after considering many aspects of the real estate development project like space availability, urban density, activity mapping, and age cohort studies. For one-north, the standard planning ratios are obtained from Singapore's Jurong Town Corporation (JTC) detailed land use plans, which take account cost aspects prior to generating the zoning maps (JTC, 2010).

According to Jurong Town Corporation (JTC), the expected population at one-north ranges from a hundred thousand to two hundred thousand people (i.e., residents and workers) by the end of nearly thirty years (2003–2030). The Jurong Town Corporation's (JTC) detailed land use plan allocates gross floor ratio (GFA) for parks, retail, sports, and recreation as shown in table 6.2. Assuming the minimum one hundred thousand figure, if one simply divides the total allocated space of secondary land uses by the expected population, we can obtain the minimum space required for park, retail, recreation, and sports per person for the two-hundred-hectare urban site. This can be used as a constant planning ratio to service the population of primary agents.

Therefore, the subsidiary agents of the KBUD-LUDM are initialised in the ratio of table 6.3. For clarification, take the example that where there are ten technology firms located in a land unit, and with respect to the earlier table 6.2, then each technology firm (i.e., agent), on an average, consists of fifteen people.

Table 6.3. Assumptions for secondary agents in the agent initialisation procedure (AIP)

Variable name	Residents	Green space/ Parks	Retail	Sports and recreation
Expected population @ One north[1]	100,000			
GFA – Total planned development (sq m)[2]		1,35,466	1,10,023	1,09,302
Space per person (sq m)		1.35	1.1	1.09
Approximated GFA		1,35,000	1,10,000	1,09,000
Percentage deviation				
Secondary agents planning ratio (minimum space required per person)		Agent 2 sq m	Agent 1.1 sq m	Agent 1.09 sq m

Source: JTC; author (2020).

The total space demand of the subsidiary (secondary) agents for the following land uses is estimated:

$Parks = 300$ sq m $(10 \times 15 \times 2$ sq m$)$ (6.2)
$Retail = 165$ sq m $(10 \times 15 \times 1.1$ sq m$)$ (6.3)
$Sports\ and\ recreation = 163.5$ sq m $(10 \times 15 \times 1.09$ sq m$)$ (6.4)

In the agent-based model, a secondary agent is created for every primary agent, with an intrinsic value of the minimum space requirement; similarly for parks and green space where fifteen agents, each with two-square-meter space requirement is initialised.

Housing needs are essential to sustain a twenty-four-hour vibrancy in any urban development project. Empirical studies find that knowledge-based workers tend to locate much closer to their workplaces, mainly attributed to the non-routine type of work patterns associated with their jobs. Post-industrial districts are gearing

PROJECT MANAGEMENT – AN ARTIFICIAL INTELLIGENT (AI) APPROACH

towards live-work-play designs to be compatible with workers' non-routine nature by providing amenities and, mainly, housing closer to work. The master plan of the Singapore's one-north KBUD aims to house 30 per cent of its workers within the two-hundred-hectare site to enable a work-life balance. While this may not seem much, it is important to note that Singapore is 100 per cent urbanised and that one-north is surrounded by public and private estates servicing the workers on-site.

Table 6.4 shows the different types of housing that are planned to accommodate one-north's population. The housing types comprise apartments or condominium units, detached housing, and semi-detached housing. As land is scarce and expensive in Singapore, condominiums and apartments satisfy most of one-north's housing needs at about 20 per cent of the resident population. Semi-detached and detached housing are deemed for dual live-work purposes to service a mere 10 per cent of the total resident population.

Table 6.4. Assumptions for secondary agents (housing only) in the agent initialisation procedure (AIP)

Agent	Type of housing	Percentage of residents serviced (%)	Number of people serviced	Space per person (sq ft)	Total space per agent (sq ft)
Housing	Apartment/condominium	20	3	350	1,200
	Detached housing	5	4	500	2,000
	Semi-detached housing	5	6	300	1,800

Source: Author (2020).

A simplified example is to assume that fifteen technology firms are planned on-site. As there are a total of 150 workers, the number of apartment units needed is thirty units, requiring the gross floor area (GFA) of 31,500 sq ft. The space requirement is imputed for detached housing and semi-detached housing to be 15,000 sq ft and 13,500 sq ft, respectively.

Apartment/condominium = 36,000 *GFA* ((10×(15×0.20))×1,200   (6.5)
Detached housing = 15,000 *GFA* ((10×(15×0.05)))×2,000   (6.6)
Semi-detached housing = 13,500 *GFA* ((10×(15×0.05)))×1,800   (6.7)

To initialise the one-north baseline model, the KBUD-LUDM planning model seeks to simulate future scenarios. The stipulated assumptions are the starting point to demonstrate the model's capacity to generate optimal design solutions. The associated knowledge interaction design criteria (KIDC) and the land use cost criteria (LUCC) are adopted. It is noteworthy that the planning ratios are secondary agents and do not need to be static. They can be changed to suit their unique future developmental requirements.

Scenario Planning

Traditional master planning for urban development often relies on professional expertise to achieve well-defined urban design goal, which ensures the sustenance of the physical structure of the plan over time. However, urban planners often face changing local conditions and uncertain economic climates, which force them to handle extraordinary surprises that detract the development from its intended goals (Scott 1998). Planners at Singapore's one-north KBUD face changing local conditions and uncertain economic climates during the conceptual phase years. There are associated costs; with the absence of demand for one or more land uses, stipulated in one-north's master plan. Old land use maps are discarded, while new land use designs are redrawn to suit prevailing economic conditions. Such redrawing of new land use designs seem unplanned 'on the fly', as one planner recounted, but leaving much room for the original land use designs to be adjusted.

Planning for the future can have different variations, according due risk to the planner's project. Peterson et al. (2003) classify such project risk to be interacting phases, depending on the uncertainty and controllability during the planning process. For one-north, its large-scale post-industrial cluster developments are riddled with high uncertainty and low controllability, owing to demand changes that are influenced by local and global economic forces. Scenario planning should therefore be adopted to take account of a variety of possible outcomes, which equips the planner with alternative scenarios to deal with uncertainty and to develop more resilient conservation policies but retaining the original design goals. Resultant projections help the planner to recommend appropriate decisions under uncontrollable and irreducible uncertainties.

Fig. 6.4. Scenario planning for the one-north knowledge-based urban development-land use design model (KBUD-LUDM)

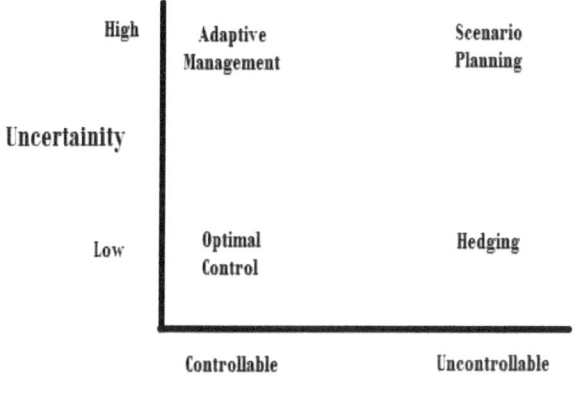

Source: Peterson et al. (2003); author (2020).

It is essential to emphasise that the KBUD-LUDM of figure 6.5 is unlike many land use models. The KBUD-LUDM is not a predictive model but merely a projection model. In this predictive model, future events are 'predicted' using basic understanding of the prevailing drivers and reasonable parameter assumptions of those drivers, given their probability distributions (Clark et al. 2001). Scenario planning for the KBUD-LUDM is conducted in practice with a small group of research scientists, managers, policymakers, and other essential stakeholders through an iterative process (Peterson et al. 2003).

To facilitate scenario planning, a storyline is adopted in line with the intentions of the official master plan. Future projections of one-north is provided in table 6.5. To account for the different planned scenarios, a set of simulations is conducted. Future scenarios should be sufficiently distinct from one another to reflect the scenario planning model's flexibility. Such a model can freeze the assumptions of the baseline scenario for the one-north KBUD-LUDM. The model then builds, via an incremental planning approach, the multiple future scenarios.

The baseline scenario is simulated as the benchmark for the one-north KBUD-LUDM of table 6.5 and with all three phases of the Biopolis and Fusionopolis complexes completed. The baseline scenario is simulated for phases one and two, where the total number of workers are estimated at about 23,600 workers; and that the workers demand a total workspace of 254,555 sqm for the combined Biopolis and Fusionopolis complexes. Information concerning how many institutions, technology firms, service firms, and university departments, along with their fields of interest and their space they occupy, would inform the agent initialisation procedure (AIP). The information is close to the survey data that is collected via consultations with senior planners of one-north's planning team of table 6.6.

For the baseline, reasonable assumptions are made after obtaining expert opinion from one-north's senior planners at the Jurong Town Corporation (JTC). Minimum planning standards that enable the KBUD-LUDM to estimate the land use demand from incoming agents as shown in table 6.7. The first column shows the primary agent classification and the minimum unit of representation by their respective type. To be followed is the number of workers, the minimum space, and the number of agents planned on-site for the baseline scenario in the second, third, and fourth columns.

Table 6.5. Future planning scenarios of one-north for the knowledge-based urban development-land use design model (KBUD-LUDM)

Time horizon (in years)	Planning scenario	Agent initialisation procedure [AIP]			
		Number of agents per scenario	Agent Kb Ratio	Organisational type	Public-private ratio
2003–2009	Optimistic (Baseline)	2000	$\alpha=0.5, \beta=0.5, \gamma=0$	$TF = 0.30, RI = 0.50,$ $EI = 0.10, SF = 0.10$	80:20
2012	Pessimistic	600	$\alpha=0.40, \beta=0.40, \gamma=0.20$	$TF = 0.25, RI = 0.45,$ $EI = 0.20, SF = 0.10$	70:30
2015	Pessimistic	1000	$\alpha=0.30, \beta=0.30, \gamma=0.40$	$TF = 0.20, RI = 0.30,$ $EI = 0.15, SF = 0.35$	60:40
2018	Neutral	1600	$\alpha=0.25, \beta=0.25, \gamma=0.50$	$TF = 0.40, RI = 0.10,$ $EI = 0.10, SF = 0.40$	50:50
2021	Optimistic	2500	$\alpha=0.15, \beta=0.25, \gamma=0.60$	$TF = 0.30, RI = 0.30,$ $EI = 0.30, SF = 0.10$	40:60
2024	Optimistic	3500	$\alpha=0.25, \beta=0.25, \gamma=0.50$	$TF = 0.40, RI = 0.15,$ $EI = 0.15, SF = 0.30$	30:70

Source: Author (2020).

NB: The baseline is informed from past estimations of the number of actors accommodated at one-north between 2003 and 2009.

Table 6.6. Space allocation of the phase one development of the one-north KBUD

Cluster name	Space provided	Number of workers (approximately)	Year of completion
Biopolis			
Phase 1	185,000 m²	4,500	2009
Phase 2	37,000 m²	1,000	2012
Phase 3	41,505 m²	1,000	2015
Fusionopolis			
Phase 1	120,000 m²	6,000	2010
Phase 2B	103,635 m²	5,000	2013
Phase 2A	50,000 m²	5,000	2010
Total		22,500	

Source: JTC official website; author (2020).

Table 6.7. Baseline agent initialisation procedure (AIP) assumptions[7]

Agent type [MUR[8]]	Number of workers	Minimum space required per person (sq ft)	Number of agents	Total space required (sq m)	Estimated number of workers
Technology firm [firm]	15	120	600	100,335	9,000
Research institution [department]	10	120	1000	111,484	10,000
Educational [department] (e.g., university, school, etc.)	10	100	200	18,581	2,000
Services [firm]	13	100	200	24,155	2,600
Total	NA	NA	1,000	254,555[9]	23,600

Figure 6.6 is the pie chart of the split up of the primary agents by organisation type of one-north and its baseline scenario.

---

[7] Planning ratios in table 5.6 were obtained through expert opinion from the head of the one-north planning team. These follow from local industrial planning practices.

[8] MUR - minimum unit of representation.

[9] This figure shows the demand for space only from primary agents.

Fig. 6.6. Distribution Assumptions of Primary Agents at One-North for the Knowledge-Based Urban Development Land Use Design Model (KBUD-LUDM) and the Baseline Scenario

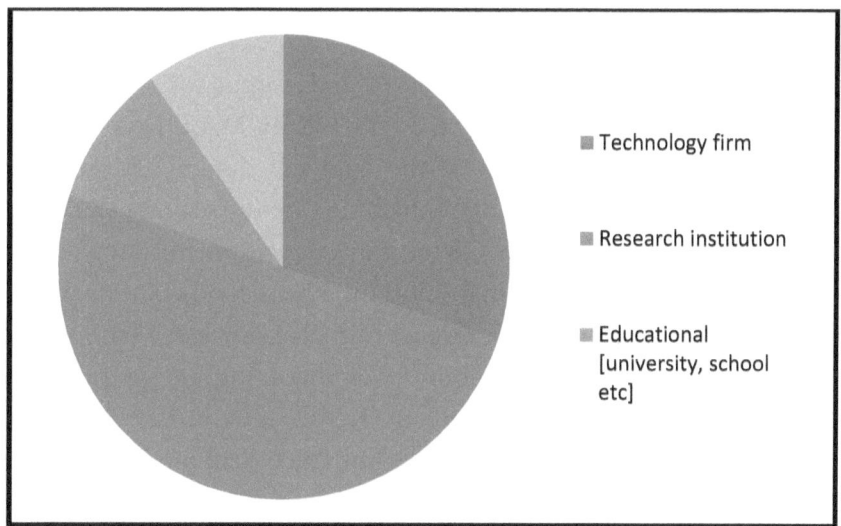

Source: Author (2020).

After several interviews with senior planners of the one-north planning team, an approximate distribution is assumed for one-north's biomedical, engineering, and sciences firms. Attempts are made to empirically validate the approximations of table 6.8 by comparing them with the tenant statistics of one-north. From survey data, simple assumptions are made with respect to the knowledge base distribution of one-north. For example, phase one assumes that 50 per cent of the primary agents has an analytical knowledge base, while the other 50 per cent has a synthetic knowledge base of the media and arts complex (i.e., the Mediapolis complex). It is explicit that the Biopolis is the biomedical cluster, which is involved with the more basic and industrial research activities. The Fusionopolis is involved with the applied physical sciences and engineering cluster.[20] It is also assumed that 80 per cent of the primary agents belong to the public institutions because the Singapore government houses most research institutions at one-north's phases one and two, to so anchor future private investments.

The One-North Baseline Simulation Results

The KBUD-LUDM specification and output for the baseline scenario is provided in table 6.8. The KBUD-LUDM reaches a solution in the first round of the land use design optimisation procedure using the knowledge interaction design criteria (KIDC).

The first column in table 6.8 indicates the number of simulations (i.e., trials) to reach an optimal solution. The second column shows the percentage of actors with respect to their knowledge base—that is, the knowledge base distribution of incoming agents into the knowledge-based urban development (KBUD). In the first decade of one-north's development, only phases one and two of the Biopolis and Fusionopolis complexes are built. The Biopolis complex is envisioned by the Jurong Town Corporation (JTC) to be the core biomedical research facility, conducting basic and applied scientific research that fall under the realm of the analytical base. The Fusionopolis complex is envisioned to be Singapore's research and development (R & D) hub for information technology, communications, media, the physical sciences, and engineering. It is inferred that the Fusionopolis complex houses mostly the synthetic type of actors.

The third knowledge-based cluster hosting symbolic agents is the Mediapolis complex. The first building of the Mediapolis complex commences construction only in February of 2011[21]; the symbolic agents are included for scenario analysis of one-north's future development at one-north. In the second column of table 6.8, the agents are split equally between the analytical and synthetic knowledge bases ($\alpha = 0.5$, $\beta = 0.5$), leaving the symbolic agents out of the baseline scenario ($\gamma = 0$). The key empirical output variables, ∂_G and σ_G, in their final stages are 0.56 and 0.25, respectively.

PROJECT MANAGEMENT – AN ARTIFICIAL INTELLIGENT (AI) APPROACH

Table 6.8. Land use optimisation results for baseline scenario adopting the knowledge-based urban development-land use design model (KBUD-LUDM)

Simulation trials	Kb ratio	Agents	Global delta (∂_G)	Target $\partial_G \sim 0.50$	Std. deviation σ_G	Optimal design solution
1	α=0.5, β=0.5, γ=0	2,000	∂_{KB} = 0.63, ∂_{org} = 0.61, ∂_{inst} = 0.39	∂_G = 0.21	0.22	N
.	.	.	.	.	.	.
2,044	α=0.5, β=0.5, γ=0	2,000	∂_{KB} = 0.63, ∂_{org} = 0.61, ∂_{inst} = 0.39	∂_G = 0.56	0.25	Y

There are about 2,044 simulations (trials) carried out for the baseline KBUD-LUDM prior to reaching an optimal solution. The gradual improvement of the global delta value towards the optimum and the reduction of the standard deviation to the minima is graphed in figure 6.7.

Fig. 6.7. Graph illustrating total iterations performed using the knowledge-based urban development-land use design model (KBUD-LUDM) for the baseline scenario of the one-north KBUD, achieving optimal land use design ($\partial_G \sim 0.50$)

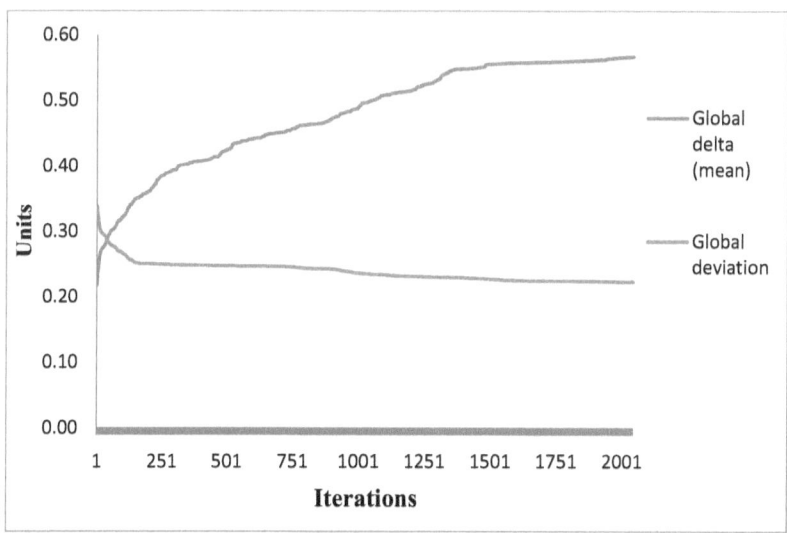

Source: Author (2020).

Illustrations of the optimal solution, which adopt the knowledge interaction design criteria (KIDC) and the land use cost criteria (LUCC), are presented in figures 6.8, 6.9, and 6.10. Figure 6.8 depicts the developmental stage of one-north by the type of institutional distribution, whereas figures 6.9 (a) and (b) capture the distribution of agents by institution and knowledge base. Figures 6.10 (a) and (b) show the land use design split by the type of agents in the planned (KBUD).

Figures 6.11 (a), (b), and (c) utilise the land use design details as input into the CityCAD® software program to produce a three-dimensional representation of the baseline scenario. The KBUD-LUDM generates the detailed land use plan for the one-north baseline scenario (see appendix). The baseline scenario demonstrates the KBUD-LUDM's ability to replicate the first two phases of one-north's development. The baseline scenario is not an exact replication of one-north but a mere demonstration of the KBUD-LUDM's ability to attain optimal land use design solutions by adopting the agent-based modelling (ABM) approach. It is noteworthy that the KBUD-LUDM is a projection model rather than a prediction or a forecast model.

Fig. 6.8. Agent–based simulation of baseline scenario, one-north (institutional colour-coded)

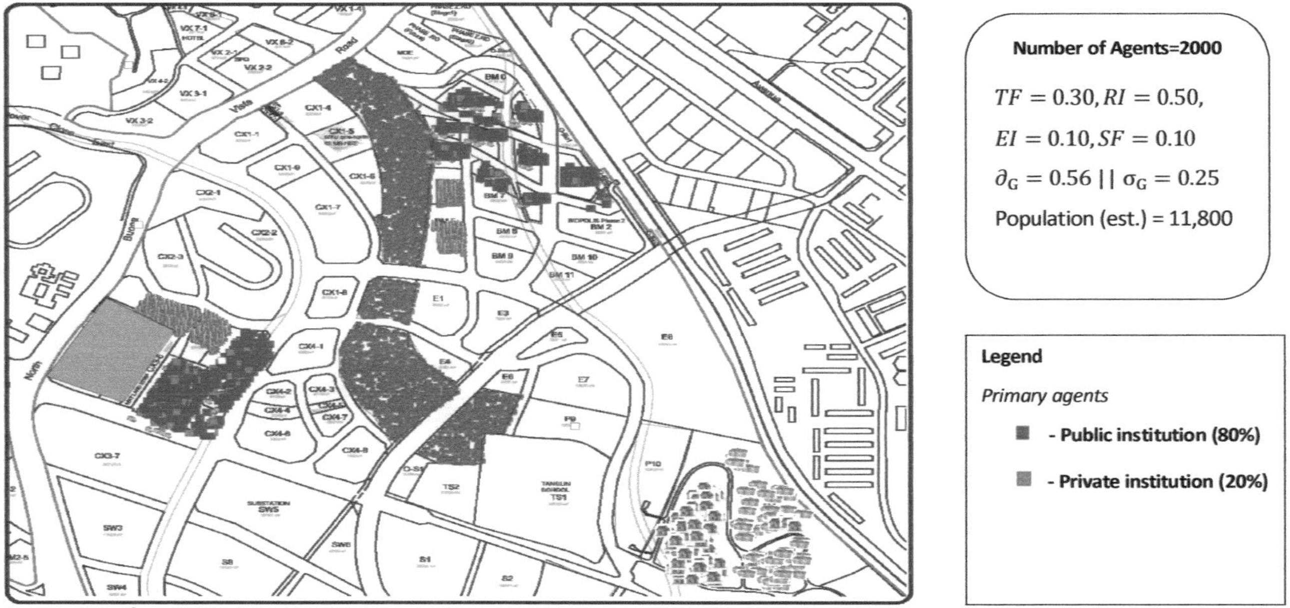

Number of Agents=2000

$TF = 0.30, RI = 0.50,$
$EI = 0.10, SF = 0.10$
$\partial_G = 0.56 \,||\, \sigma_G = 0.25$
Population (est.) = 11,800

Legend
Primary agents
■ - Public institution (80%)
■ - Private institution (20%)

Source: Author (2020).

NB: Figure 6.8 shows the optimal land use design solution that maximises knowledge interactions for all agents based on the knowledge interaction design criteria (KIDC). The baseline shows the one-north development with the Biopolis and Fusionopolis complexes.

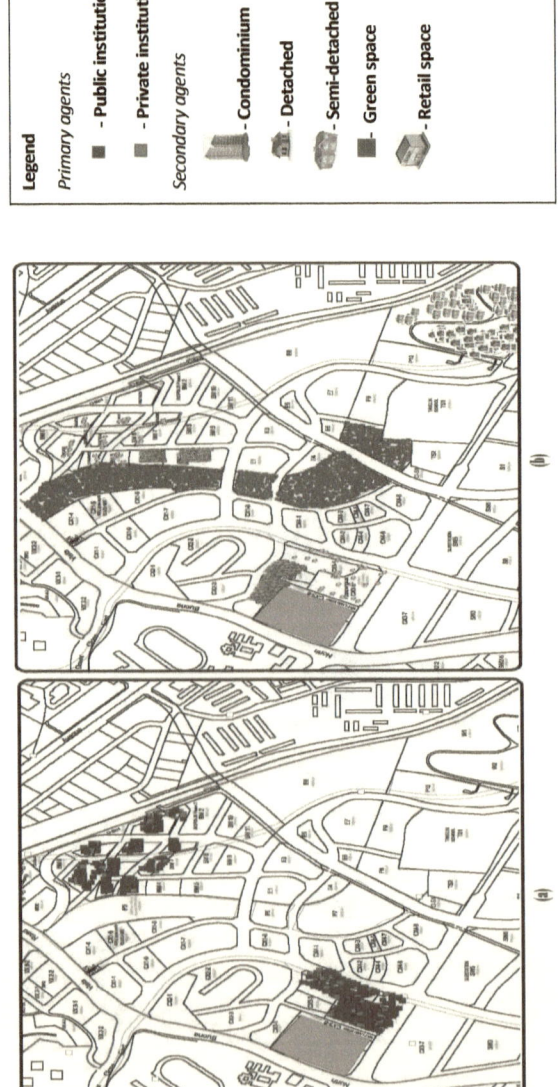

Fig. 6.9. Agent-based simulation of the baseline scenario of one-north by type of agent (primary and secondary)

Source: Author (2020)

NB: In the previous figure 6.8, the overlap of agents because of mixed-use zoning may cause difficulty in observing the different types of agents in the land use design baseline scenario of one-north. Figures 6.9 (a) and (b) show the optimal land use design solution split by primary and secondary agents, respectively, for the baseline scenario.

Fig. 6.10. Agent-based simulation of baseline scenario of one-north (knowledge and organisational base) (colour-coded)

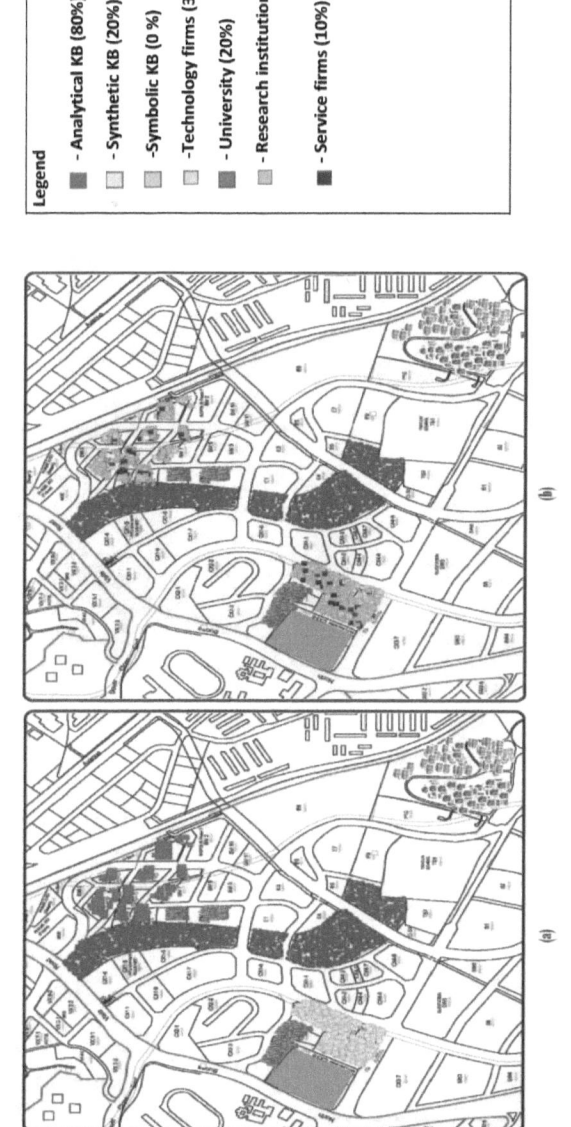

Source: Author (2020).

NB: Figures 6.10 (a) and (b) are similar to figure 6.9. However, figures 6.10 (a) and (b) are colour-coded to illustrate the mix of (a) knowledge bases and (b) organisational bases; see legend on the right-hand side. Urban planners can derive zoning maps to indicate land parcels compatible with the specific knowledge bases and organisational divisions within and between blocks, to facilitate the land use design's overall knowledge interactions and consequently facilitate the cross-fertilisation of ideas.

Fig. 6.11. Computer-aided design (CAD) extension of the knowledge-based urban development-land use design model (KBUD-LUDM) agent-based model for baseline scenario of one-north, Singapore, using CityCAD®

Source: Author (2020).

NB: Figure 6.11 represents the computer-aided design (CAD) model of the baseline agent-based model of one-north, subject to agent specification. The first image (a) gives an aerial view of the simulated three-dimensional models showing the Biopolis and the Fusionopolis complexes in their early stages of development (phase 1); (b) and (c) show more detailed three-dimensional views and with a street view of the Fusionopolis complex, as seen from the nearby Biopolis complex. The green patches represent secondary agents showing their green space distribution, and the red blocks are pre-existing institutional (educational and community) space. The rest of the grey patches are undeveloped land parcels for future urban development.

The Scenario Planning Analysis

Scenario planning is an integral part of the urban planning and development process. It helps the stakeholders realise the viability and flexibility of the land use design in times of uncertainty. The appropriate number of scenarios for planners is usually four to five. Some authors have noted that more than four to five scenarios may confuse users and constrain the stakeholders' ability to explore plausible uncertainties (Van der Heijden 1996; Wack 2002).

Scenario planning is executed on a storyline approach, where at each stage of the planning process, the planner is required to enter a set of agents—that is, information on incoming actors and their rough proportions. The scenarios are broadly classified as optimistic, pessimistic, and neutral, reflecting, say, the expected demand for space at one-north under different economic situations. Figure 6.12 depicts such three scenarios as perceived for the KBUD-LUDM.

Fig. 6.12. Scenario thresholds for one-north knowledge-based urban development–land use design model (KBUD-LUDM)

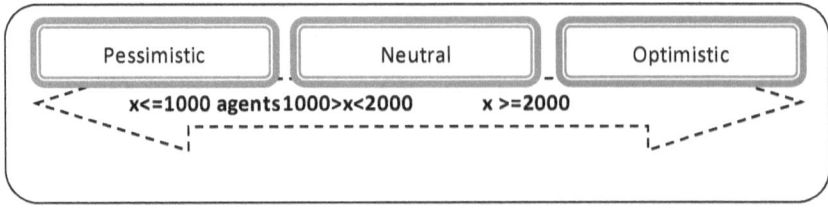

Source: Author (2020).

Table 6.9 presents the set of input and output variables for a given set of scenarios. The first column shows the time horizon in years, and the second column shows the scenario status—optimistic, neutral, and pessimistic. The first batch of tenants intakes at one-north for the baseline scenario, which is deemed to be a successful scenario amongst local urban planners in Singapore. The table shows an evolutionary picture of the simulated knowledge-based urban development-land use design model (KBUD-LUDM) agent-based model simulations at every stage of the development process.

The frequency chosen for scenario planning analysis is about three years, which gives the KBUD-LUDM an incremental planning approach, as compared to one-north's traditional master plan of thirty years. Following the baseline scenario in table 6.9, the first (pessimistic) scenario coincides with the period after the global financial crisis inclusive of crisis-struck Singapore. Urban planners expect falling space demand for the next four years (2009–2012). Such falling space demand is only planned for a fraction of agents (~30%), as compared to the earlier period (2003–2009), when a total of six hundred agents entered the knowledge-based urban development (KBUD) project. The optimal design is obtained with a global delta (∂_G) of 0.45 and a global sigma (σ_G) of 0.25, which satisfies the knowledge interaction design criteria (KIDC) of the inequality:

$$0.30 >= \partial_G <= 0.70$$

In the neutral and other scenarios, one-north experiences an influx of educational institutions and service firms, to support the existing technology firms and research institutions. The latter institutions support knowledge production, and they provide essential services to the existing tenants.

Table 6.9. The knowledge-based urban development-land use design model (KBUD-LUDM) for the multiple scenarios planning approach

Time horizon (in years)	Planning scenario	Agent initialisation procedure [AIP]				KBUD-LUDM outcome
		Number of agents per scenario	Agent Kb Ratio	Organisational type	Public-private ratio	Global delta ∂_G [sigma σ_G]
2003–2009	Optimistic (baseline)	2000	α=0.5, β=0.5, γ=0	TF=0.30, RI=0.50, EI=0.10, SF=0.10	80:20	0.56 [0.25]
2012	Pessimistic	600	α=0.40, β=0.40, γ=0.20	TF=0.25, RI=0.45, EI=0.20, SF=0.10	70:30	0.45 [0.24]
2015	Pessimistic	1000	α=0.30, β=0.30, γ=0.40	TF=0.20, RI=0.30, EI=0.15, SF=0.35	60:40	0.43 [0.19]
2018	Neutral	1600	α=0.25, β=0.25, γ=0.50	TF=0.40, RI=0.10, EI=0.10, SF=0.40	50:50	0.49 [0.33]
2021	Optimistic	2500	α=0.15, β=0.25, γ=0.60	TF=0.30, RI=0.30, EI=0.30, SF=0.10	40:60	0.46 [0.18]
2024	Optimistic	3500	α=0.25, β=0.25, γ=0.50	TF=0.40, RI=0.15, EI=0.15, SF=0.30	30:70	0.31 [0.29]

Source: Author (2020).

<u>NB:</u> In table 6.9, α, β, and γ represent the percentage of planned agents expected to belong to the analytical, synthetic, and symbolic knowledge bases. The organisational types TF,RI,EI SF represent the expected percentages of technology firms, research institutions, university (educational), and service firms.

From table 6.9, the first (pessimistic) scenario of one-north sees the launch of the Mediapolis complex cluster (γ>0) that hosts the media-, design-, and arts-related organisations. Initial demand for housing development (T1) begins, but that development does not fully occupy the available plot space. The inference is that there is a waiting period until the critical population (>50%) is reached to service the land. The second (pessimistic) scenario slightly improves and yet remains pessimistic, with space demand stifled because of poor local and global economic conditions.

The third (neutral) scenario sees slow improvement of the Singapore economy and with the inflow of actors to the Biopolis complex, Fusionopolis complex, and Mediapolis complex clusters. The Mediapolis complex cluster gains momentum via constituting a major proportion ($\gamma = 0.50$) of the incoming actors. The Biopolis complex and Fusionopolis complex clusters, which constitute the north and west parts of the one-north site, have reached about 60 per cent to 70 per cent of site occupancy.

The fourth (optimistic) scenario sees rising demand for the Mediapolis complex and the Fusionopolis complex clusters, where there is still the availability of undeveloped land to be serviced. Ten condominium housing developments in total are set to commence for immediate construction, and with a combined capacity of 5,668 units to accommodate about seventeen thousand residents is the Wessex estate, south-east of the one-north site. This Wessex estate is zoned to host landed housing and is slated for the development of 577 detached and 235 semi-detached housing units. Such an estate is proposed to accommodate 3 per cent to 4 per cent of the total household population.

From figure 6.13, public sector participation is lowered as a proportion over all the scenarios by calendar year. This is in line with the Jurong Town Corporation's (JTC) consideration that public institutes, together with public participation in general, are to merely provide an anchoring role for future private investments.

Fig. 6.13. Expected institutional participation levels over time in the scenario analysis

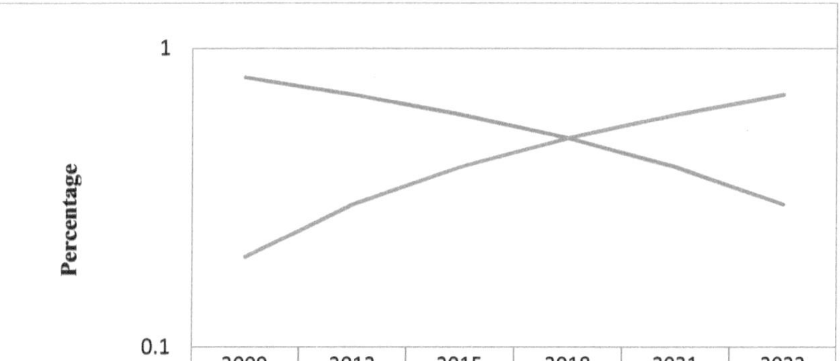

	2009	2012	2015	2018	2021	2023
Public sector	0.8	0.7	0.6	0.5	0.4	0.3
Private sector	0.2	0.3	0.4	0.5	0.6	0.7

Source: Author (2020).

The fifth (optimistic) scenario is expected to experience robust space demand for all three clusters because of improved local and global economic conditions. One-north realises a resident population of 121,640 individuals and with the percentage of the built environment at just above 50 per cent. Major on-site plots are proposed to be allocated for green spaces to compensate for the high presence of built-up spaces on-site. A number of land plots are deemed to be fit for housing development. Retail developments are incorporated to be a percentage of every building to satisfy minimum requirements set out in the earlier table 6.2. However, dedicated commercial and retail developments are also proposed for few sites near transit nodes.

Figure 6.14 depicts the evolution of the incremental planning approach for the one-north knowledge-based urban development (KBUD) project into the future. Then figure 6.15 presents the computer-aided design (CAD) model of the last, fifth, (optimistic) scenario of one-north's knowledge-based urban development-land use design model (KBUD-LUDM).

Fig. 6.14. Optimal land use designs obtained from scenario planning analysis of the one-north KBUD-LUDM

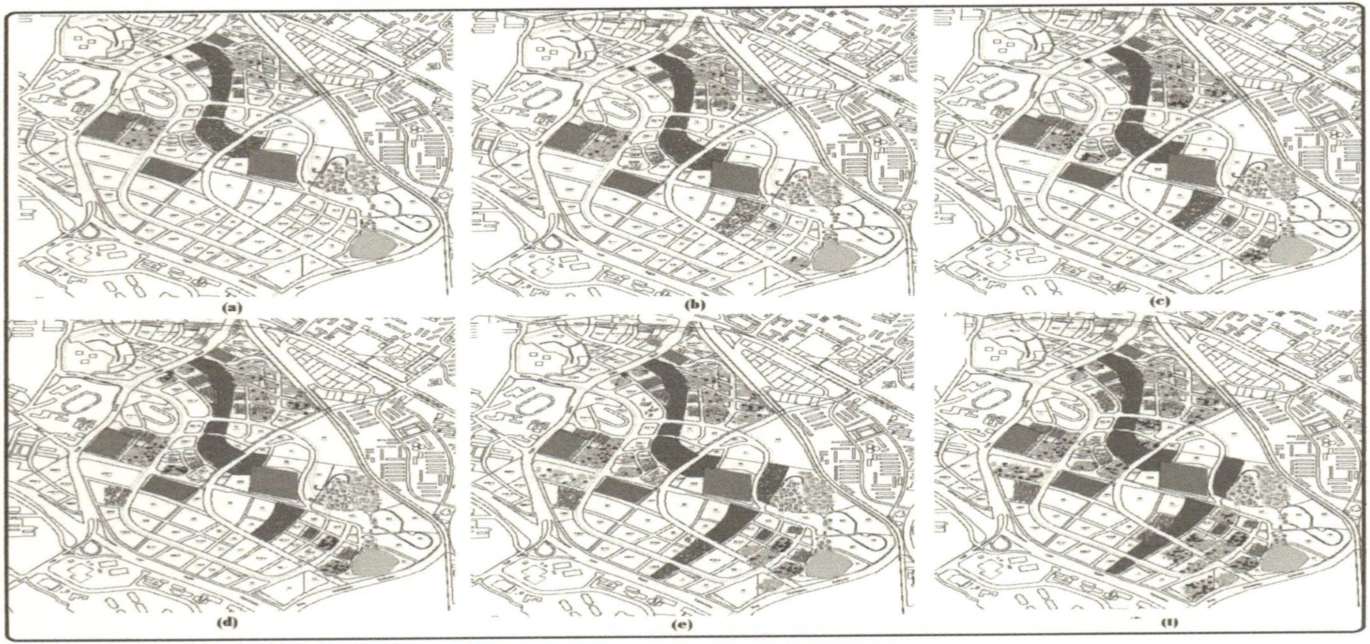

NB: The above simulation panels show the incremental planning approach for the one-north knowledge-based urban development in accordance with the AIP data of the earlier table 6.9.

Fig. 6.15. Computer-aided design (CAD) extension of the agent-based KBUD-LUDM for the final scenario (2024) of one-north, Singapore, deploying the software CityCAD®

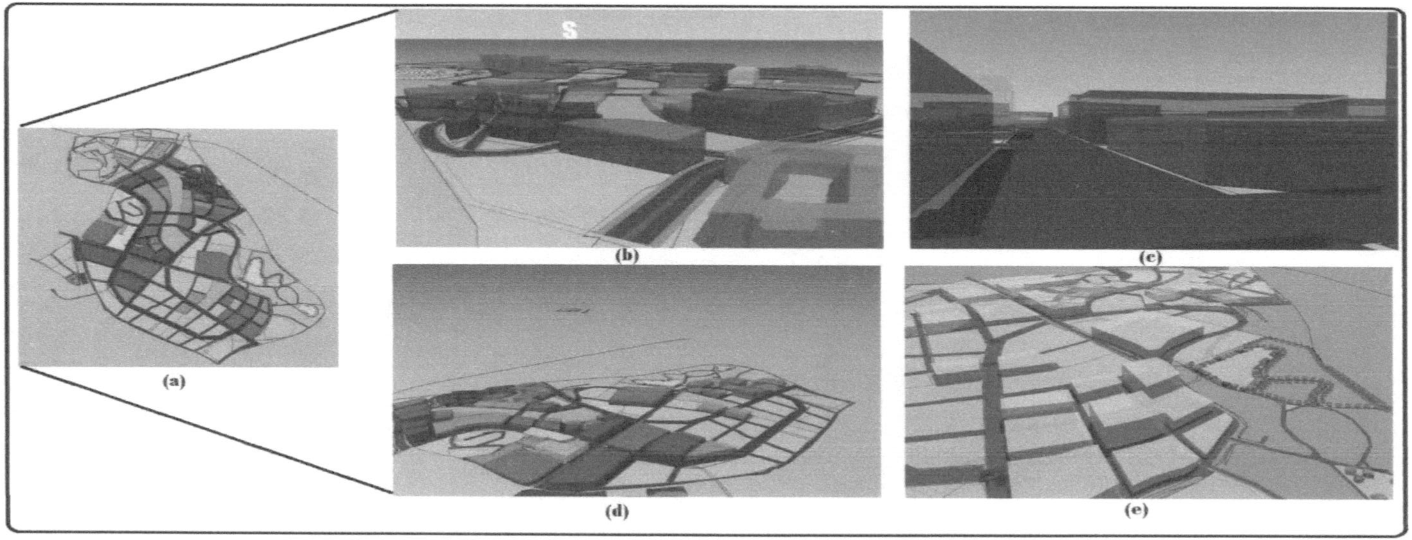

Source: Author (2020).

NB: The blue and yellow blocks are representative of one-north's land development process until the baseline scenario (see table 6.9). The purple blocks are proposed for development for all scenarios after the baseline scenario. The orange blocks are reserved for residential development. The red blocks represent existing institutional sites unavailable for development. The green strips represent land allocated for open spaces and parks. The rest are undeveloped land available for future use.

Validation Procedure

The emergence of the agent-based modelling (ABM) literature has led to rising awareness amongst modellers, to check and correct for path dependency and multiple equilibrium issues especially in economic, ecological, and spatial land use systems (Atkinson and Oleson 1996; Balmann 2001; Pahl-Wostl 1995). Path dependency arises from negative and positive feedback that reinforce each other to create large deviations from the optimal results. There is rising necessity to validate spatial land use models. Multiple equilibria are unfavourable because they raise the models' uncertainty in obtaining land use design solutions for planning purposes. One can extend these concerns to our chapter's land use design optimisation model. To get around this problem, Brown et al. (2005) suggest that modellers focus on two aspects to validate agent-based land use models. First is adopting 'aggregate similarity' followed by 'spatial similarity'. For brevity, refer to the appendix for the complete validation procedure of the KBUD-LUDM.

Concluding Remarks

City planners of the twenty-first century see the knowledge-based urban development (KBUD) strategy as a new form of urban renewal of industrial cities. They believe it can potentially bring economic, technological progress, and sustainable socio-spatial order to the contemporary city.[22] Inefficient large-scale urban designs of

PROJECT MANAGEMENT – AN ARTIFICIAL INTELLIGENT (AI) APPROACH

planned post-industrial complexes clusters have the potential to create dissociation of related activities. This resulting rise of physical barriers can lead to a reduced level of intra-cluster knowledge interactions via both planned and spontaneous channels.

Chapter 6 addresses the growing need for an urban design criterion that aids in efficient land use planning for knowledge-based urban developments (KBUDs). Apart from aesthetic benefits, the chapter discusses that planned mixed-use land use designs can help shape knowledge interactions between different types of actors by placing 'related' workers together. By exploring the literature on knowledge interactions and their determinants between different actors, one can first develop a unique urban design criterion, which is aimed at enhancing knowledge interactions (KIs) in the knowledge-based urban developments (KBUDs). This chapter defines 'actors' in the KBUDs in terms of their specific roles in the KBUD innovation ecosystem. Then drawing on important discussions from the innovation and proximity dynamics literature, one can propose what is known as the knowledge interaction design criteria (KIDC) to help urban planners associate related actors together in space. Having such a criteria satisfies one of the three important rationales stated by urban planners when performing land use zoning—that is, to integrate compatible land uses, to generate positive externalities, and to achieve mutual benefit (Chung 1994).[23]

A formal representation of a knowledge-based urban development-land use design model (KBUD-LUDM) incorporating the knowledge interaction design criteria (KIDC) is proposed, adopting agent-based methodology to obtain optimal land use design solutions. Agent-based approach is an alternative methodology to handle spatial and temporal processes, compared to the linear programming methodology, which has been used to address land use design problems.

Chapter 6's contribution to urban planning and design of the KBUD project is twofold. First, the chapter discusses how to identify and classify complementary actors in a planned post-industrial knowledge-based development project. Second, the chapter provides a dynamic alternative planning approach to 'zone' the KBUD, adopting the agent-based approach. Urban planners have long relied on land use designs informed by one-shot long-term master plans. This way has proved to be infeasible to implement, especially given the volatile nature of demand for various land uses.

The agent-based approach, which addresses the KBUDs, is meant to be an incremental planning approach to save time and resources in redesigning/rezoning efforts, under uncertain economic conditions. Promoting intra-cluster interactions by co-agglomerating knowledge-intensive actors and adopting better mixed-use zoning strategies can improve the attractiveness of the specialised direct real estate like the KBUD project in the marketplace.

Acknowledgement: *The author wishes to gratefully acknowledge the initial work carried out for chapter 6 by Dr Rengarajan, Satyanarain, a private consultant and PhD graduate (of the NUS School of Design and Environment, Department of Real Estate); and in consultation with honorary professor (University of Hertfordshire, Hatfield, UK), Dr Ho, Kim Hin / David, during their meaningful brainstorming sessions, before Professor Ho retired from the NUS School of Design and Environment Department of Real Estate in May 2019.*

References

Abukhater, A. B. E.-D. 2009. 'Rethinking planning theory and practice: a glimmer of light for Prospects of integrated planning to combat complex urban realities'. *Theoretical and Empirical Researches in Urban Management,* 4(2 (11)), 64–79.

Allen, T. J. 1984. 'Managing the flow of technology: Technology transfer and the dissemination of technological information within the R&D organization'. *MIT Press Books, 1.*

Ancona, D. G., and D. F. Caldwell. 1992. 'Bridging the boundary: External activity and performance in organizational teams'. *Administrative Science Quarterly*, 634–665.

Anselin, L., A. Varga, and Z. Acs. 1997. 'Local geographic spillovers between university research and high technology innovations'. *Journal of Urban Economics, 42*(3), 422–448.

Asheim, and M. Gertler. 2005. 'The geography of innovation'. *The Oxford Handbook of Innovation*, 291–317.

Asheim, B., L. Coenen, and J. Vang. 2007. 'Face-to-face, buzz, and knowledge bases: sociospatial implications for learning, innovation, and innovation policy'. *Environment and Planning C, 25*(5), 655.

Bajracharya, B., and L. I. J. Too. 2009. 'Developing Knowledge Precincts in Regional Towns: Opportunities and Challenges'. Chapter 6 presented at the Second International Urban Design.

Barber, G. 1976. 'Land-use plan design via interactive multiple-objective programming'. *Environment and Planning A, 8*(6), 625–636.

Bathelt, H., A. Malmberg, and P. Maskell. 2004. 'Clusters and knowledge: local buzz, global pipelines and the process of knowledge creation'. *Progress in Human geography, 28*(1), 31–56.

Batty, M. 2003. 'Agent-based pedestrian modelling'. *Advanced Spatial Analysis: The CASA Book of GIS*, 81–106.

Boschma, R. 2005. 'Proximity and innovation: a critical assessment'. *Regional Studies, 39*(1), 61–74.

Bottazzi, L., and G. Peri. 2003. 'Innovation and spillovers in regions: Evidence from European patent data'. *European Economic Review, 47*(4), 687–710.

Cantwell, J., and G. D. Santangelo. 2003. 'The new geography of corporate research in information and communications technology (ICT)'. *Change, Transformation and Development* (pp. 343–377): Springer.

Carrillo, F. J. 2004. 'Capital cities: a taxonomy of capital accounts for knowledge cities'. *Journal of Knowledge Management, 8*(5), 28–46.

Chatzkel, J. 2004. 'Greater Phoenix as a knowledge capital'. *Journal of Knowledge Management, 8*(5), 61–72.

Cheng, P., C. J. Choi, S. Chen, T. I. Eldomiaty, and C. C. Millar. 2004. 'Knowledge repositories in knowledge cities: institutions, conventions and knowledge subnetworks'. *Journal of Knowledge Management, 8*(5), 96–106.

Cohen, W. M., and D. A. Levinthal. 1990. 'Absorptive capacity: a new perspective on learning and innovation'. *Administrative Science Quarterly*, 128–152.

Cooke, P. 2001. 'Regional innovation systems, clusters, and the knowledge economy'. *Industrial and Corporate Change, 10*(4), 945–974.

Cooke, P., M. G. Uranga, and G. Etxebarria. 1998. 'Regional systems of innovation: an evolutionary perspective'. *Environment and Planning A, 30*, 1563–1584.

Correia, P., and M. Madden. 1985. 'Optimisation of land purchasing and management using mixed integer programming: a case study in a Portuguese municipal authority'. *Environment and Planning B: Planning and Design, 12*(3), 335–349.

den Hertog, P. 2002. 'Co-producers of innovation: on the role of knowledge-intensive business services in innovation'. *Productivity, Innovation and Knowledge in Services: New Economic and Socio-Economic Approaches*, 223.

Dresner, K., and P. Stone, P. 2004. 'Multiagent traffic management: A reservation-based intersection control mechanism'. Chapter 6 presented at the proceedings of the Third International Joint Conference on Autonomous Agents and Multiagent Systems-Volume 2.

Duffy, F., D. Jaunzens, A. Laing, and S. Willis. 2012. *New Environments for Working*: Taylor & Francis.

Elfring, T., and W. Hulsink. 2003. 'Networks in entrepreneurship: the case of high-technology firms'. *Small Business Economics, 21*(4), 409–422.

Etzkowitz, H., and L. Leydesdorff. 2000. 'The dynamics of innovation: from National Systems and "Mode 2" to a Triple Helix of university-industry-government relations'. *Research Policy, 29*(2), 109–123.

Foray, D. 2005. 'Economic fundamentals of the knowledge society'. *Informationsgesellschaft. Geschichten und Wirklichkeit. Fribourg. S*, 211–240.

Fox, M. S., M. Barbuceanu, and R. Teigen. 2000. 'Agent-oriented supply-chain management'. *International Journal of Flexible Manufacturing Systems, 12*(2-3), 165–188.

Garcia, B. C. 2004. 'Developing futures: a knowledge-based capital for Manchester'. *Journal of Knowledge Management, 8*(5), 47–60.

Hertog, P. D. 2000. 'Knowledge-intensive business services as co-producers of innovation'. *International Journal of Innovation Management, 4*(04), 491–528.

Hillier, B., P. O'Sullivan, A. Penn M. Kolokotroni, M. Rasmussen, and J. Xu. 1990. *The Design of Research Laboratories*.

Hughes, H. P., C. W. Clegg, M. A. Robinson, and R. M. Crowder. 2012. 'Agent-based modelling and simulation: The potential contribution to organizational psychology'. *Journal of Occupational and Organizational Psychology, 85*(3), 487–502.

Isaksen, A. 2004. 'Knowledge-based clusters and urban location: the clustering of software consultancy in Oslo'. *Urban Studies, 41*(5-6), 1157–1174.

Janssen, R., M. van Herwijnen, T. J. Stewart, and J. Aerts. 2008. 'Multiobjective decision support for land-use planning'. *Environment and Planning B Planning and Design, 35*(4), 740.

Kesidou, E., M. C. Caniëls, and H. A. Romijn. 2009. 'Local Knowledge Spillovers and Development: An Exploration of the Software Cluster in Uruguay: Research Chapter 6'. *Industry and Innovation, 16*(2), 247–272.

Knight, R. V. 1995. 'Knowledge-based development: policy and planning implications for cities'. *Urban Studies, 32*(2), 225–260.

Lawson, C., and E. Lorenz. 1999. 'Collective learning, tacit knowledge and regional innovative capacity'. *Regional Studies, 33*(4), 305–317.

Levitt, B., and J. G. March. 1988. 'Organizational learning'. *Annual Review of Sociology*, 319–340.

Ligtenberg, A., M. Wachowicz, A. K. Bregt, A. Beulens, and D. L. Kettenis. 2004. 'A design and application of a multi-agent system for simulation of multi-actor spatial planning'. *Journal of Environmental Management, 72*(1), 43–55.

Makowski, D., E. M. Hendrix, M. K. van Ittersum, and W. A. Rossing. 2000. 'A framework to study nearly optimal solutions of linear programming models developed for agricultural land use exploration'. *Ecological Modelling, 131*(1), 65–77.

Malmberg, A., and P. Maskell. 2006. 'Localized learning revisited'. *Growth and Change, 37*(1), 1–18.

Mascitelli, R. 2000. 'From experience: harnessing tacit knowledge to achieve breakthrough innovation'. *Journal of Product Innovation Management, 17*(3), 179–193.

Meeus, M., L. Oerlemans, and J. Hage. 2004. 'Industry-public knowledge infrastructure interaction: intra-and inter-organizational explanations of interactive learning'. *Industry and Innovation, 11*(4), 327–352.

Moodysson, J., L. Coenen, and B. Asheim. 2008. 'Explaining spatial patterns of innovation: analytical and synthetic modes of knowledge creation in the Medicon Valley life-science cluster'. *Environment and Planning A, 40*(5), 1040–1056.

Muller, E., and A. Zenker. 2001a. 'Business services as actors of knowledge transformation: the role of KIBS in regional and national innovation systems'. *Research Policy, 30*(9), 1501–1516.

Muller, E., and A. Zenker. 2001b. 'Business services as actors of knowledge transformation: the role of KIBS in regional and national innovation systems'. *Research Policy, 30*(9), 2.

Niu, X., G. McCalla, and J. Vassileva. 2003. 'Purpose-based user modelling in a multi-agent portfolio management system'. *User Modeling 2003* (pp. 398–402): Springer.

Oerlemans, L. A., M. T. Meeus, and F. W. Boekema. 2001. 'Firm clustering and innovation: Determinants and effects★'. Chapter 6s in *Regional Science, 80*(3), 337–356.

Opdam, P., E. Steingröver, and S. V. Rooij. 2006. 'Ecological networks: a spatial concept for multi-actor planning of sustainable landscapes'. *Landscape and Urban Planning, 75*(3), 322–332.

Rashid, M., K. Kampschroer, and C. Zimring. 2006. 'Spatial layout and face-to-face interaction in offices-a study of the mechanisms of spatial effects on face-to-face interaction'. *Environment and Planning B Planning and Design, 33*(6), 825.

Rees, J., and H. A. Stafford. 1986. 'Location: their relevance for understanding high-technology complexes'. *Technology, Regions, and Policy*, 23.

Said, L. B., T. Bouron, and A. Drogoul. 2002. 'Agent-based interaction analysis of consumer behavior'. Chapter 6 presented at the proceedings of the First International Joint Conference on Autonomous Agents and Multiagent Systems: part 1.

Salter, A., and D. Gann. 2003. 'Sources of ideas for innovation in engineering design'. *Research Policy, 32*(8), 1309–1324.

Sarimin, M., and T. Yigitcanlar. 2011. 'Knowledge-based urban development of Multimedia Super Corridor, Malaysia: an overview'. *International Journal of Knowledge-Based Development, 2*(1), 34–48.

Searle, G., and B. Pritchard. 2008. *Beyond Planning: Sydney's Knowledge Sector Development.*

Segal, N. S., R. Smilor, G. Kozmetsky, and D. Gibson. 1988. 'The Cambridge Phenomenon: universities, research, and local economic development in Great Britain'. *Creating the Technopolis. Ballinger, Cambridge (Massachusetts)*, 81–90.

Shaw, A. T., and J. P. Gilly. 2000. 'On the analytical dimension of proximity dynamics'. *Regional Studies, 34*(2), 169–180.

Simon, H. A. 1955. 'A behavioral model of rational choice'. *The Quarterly Journal of Economics, 69*(1), 99–118.

Torre, A., and A. Rallet. 2005. 'Proximity and localization'. *Regional Studies, 39*(1), 47–59.

Wigand, R. T. 1988. 'High technology development in the Phoenix area: Taming the desert'. *Creating the Technopolis. Ballinger, Cambridge (Massachusetts)*, 185–202.

Williams, J. C., C. S. ReVelle, and S. A. Levin. 2004. 'Using mathematical optimization models to design nature reserves'. *Frontiers in Ecology and the Environment, 2*(2), 98–105.

Yigitcanlar, T. 2009. 'Planning for knowledge-based urban development: global perspectives'. *Journal of Knowledge Management, 13*(5), 228–242.

Other Relevant Publications

Rengarajan, Satyanarain, and Kim Hin / David Ho. 2013. 'A new approach to design the Knowledge Based Urban Development (KBUD) using Agent Based Modeling'. [Chapter 6 presented European Real Estate Society Annual Conference 2013 in Vienna.] This chapter 6 has been revised and resubmitted to the *Journal of European Real Estate Research (JERR)*.

Rengarajan, Satyanarain, and Kim Hin / David Ho. 2014. 'Agent based simulation of the Knowledge Based Urban Development (KBUD): One north land use design (LUD) optimization model'. [working chapter 6]

Forthcoming

'A new approach to design the Knowledge Based Urban Development (KBUD) using Agent Based Modeling'. [Chapter 6 presented European Real Estate Society Annual Conference 2013 in Vienna. This chapter 6 has been submitted to the *Journal of European Real Estate Research (JERR)*] (Aug 2013).

Authors: Rengarajan, Satyanarain; Ho, Kim Hin / David.

'Strategic Behavioral Pricing of the Private Residential Development Market—a Simplified Experimental Approach'. This chapter 6 has been submitted to *International Journal of Housing Markets and Analysis* (Aug 2013).

Authors: Ho, Kim Hin / David; Rengarajan, Satyanarain; Hui, Chi Man / Eddie; Ho, Tai Wing.

'Industrial Real Estate Market Dynamics in Singapore: A VAR Approach'. [The chapter 6 was presented at the AsRES-AREUEA Joint International Conference 2012, Singapore]. This chapter 6 has been submitted to *Journal of Real Estate Portfolio Management* for peer review.

Authors: Ho, Kim Hin / David; Rengarajan, Satyanarain.

'Strategic industrial real estate in the new economy: the Biopolis, the Singapore experience.' Chapter 6 has been submitted to *Urban Studies* for peer review (May 2013).

Authors: Ho, Kim Hin / David; Rengarajan, Satyanarain.

'An Examination of the Structure and Dynamics of Singapore's Maturing Central Area Office Sector'. This chapter 6 has been submitted to *Urban Studies* for peer review (May 2013).

Authors: Ho, Kim Hin / David; Glascock, John L.; Rengarajan, Satyanarain.

Published

Ho, K. H. D., S. Rengarajan, and Y. H. Lum. 2013. 'Green' buildings and REIT (Real Estate Investment Trust)'s Performance'. *Journal of Property Investment & Finance*, 31(6), 3–3.

Appendix

The HAT (Heterogeneity, Adaptability, Tractability) Framework

The Heterogeneity, Adaptability, and Tractability (HAT) framework broadly provides the necessary requirements to construct and benchmark an agent based-land use model (AB-LUM) to produce tractable scenarios of the knowledge-based urban developments (KBUDs). The heterogeneity, adaptability, and tractability (HAT) framework was proposed by Arika Ligmann-Zielinska and Piotr Jankowski (2007) in their chapter 6, which examines a generic robust framework for developing reliable agent-based models. The benchmark simply reflects one vision of a good, operational planning support model that balances scientific rigor and practical manipulability (Couclelis 2002). It by no means represents the only plausible framework. The various components of the conceptual heterogeneity, adaptability, and tractability' (HAT) model framework are provided in figure 1.

Heterogeneity is a key characteristic of complex adaptive systems (CAS) that are often modelled with agent-based modelling systems (ABMS) (Benenson and Torrens 2004; Bernard 2002). In the agent-based models and as the different types of agents are introduced to represent multiple interests, the diversified actors such as the multiple developers and residents/tenants are defined.

Fig. 1. Conceptual representation of the heterogeneity, adaptability, and tractability (HAT) framework

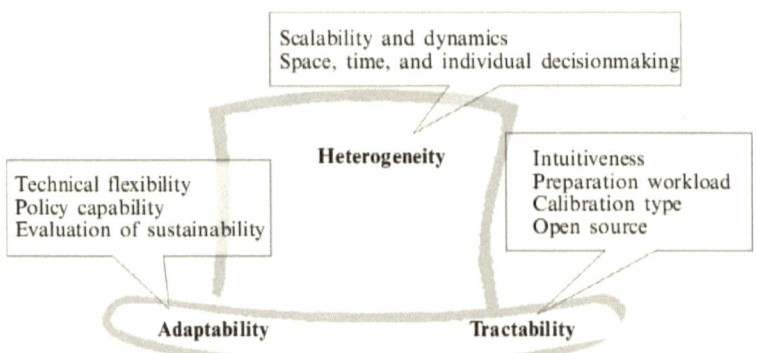

Source: Ligmann-Zielinska and Jankowski (2007); author (2020).

Heterogeneity can also be introduced into the system under study through the following:

1. differential time steps;
2. spatial (environment) variability;
3. dynamic hierarchies of system actors (e.g., the different types of organisations or family structures).

While urban modelling inevitably entails the consideration of explicit spatial variables (Berger et al. 2002a), previous land use design models have been incapable of three-dimensional representation and manipulation (Wright, Kim, and Wiggins 1989). The heterogeneity, adaptability, and tractability (HAT) framework requires the agent-based modelling systems (ABMS) models to include four spatial scalability components:

i. model abstraction—that is, the vector;
ii. representation—that is, the spatial and tabular input data sets to be included in the model (e.g., land use, zoning, vegetation);

iii. resolution—that is, the smallest homogeneous spatial unit of analysis;
iv. extent, covering the geographical location analysed.

The last component of the heterogeneity arm of the heterogeneity, adaptability, and tractability (HAT) framework is the notion of the agency in setting up an agent-based modelling systems (ABMS). Agency represents a counterpart of a real-world actor, be it animate (householder, developer, bird) or inanimate (car, house, business). If the model is set up to include different types of individuals (e.g., as owners, renters) but ignores the higher-level social structures such as families, then we are dealing with only the horizontal variety (weak agency) as opposed to the vertical variety (strong agency). When the model includes the social hierarchy (Benenson and Torrens 2004) such as the parent agents and the child agents, who build family agents over time, then we have a strong agency. This agent scalability reflects the roles played by individuals in shaping the urban environment. The agent-based models often include interactive agents with a simplified internal structure that is adequate for the characterisation of qualitative changes in spatial patterns. In summary, the agent-based model heterogeneity needs to consist of three dimensions—namely, time, space, and human decision-making (DS function) as defined by Agarwal, Green, Grove, Evans, and Schweik (2002).

Adaptability refers to the ability of the model to allow for adjustments to the specific needs of geographic place, the problem to be resolved, and the planning and design analysis phase. The heterogeneity, adaptability, and tractability (HAT) framework's adaptability arm consists of the assessment indicators such as technical flexibility, policy capability, and the evaluation of sustainability. A flexible agent-based modelling systems (ABMS) model should possess an easy interface with other models for the economic, environmental, and impact analysis. The level of software in coupling with other formats such as the standardised GIS/AutoCAD output file formats should be possible for useful examination (Boyd and Chan 2002).

For the model to be useful for practical purposes, the modeller may include the diversity of policy variables. One can follow the policy categorisation of land use models (Meyer and Miller 2001) in which the policy variables can be divided into five categories depending on their purpose. These categories are as follows:

1. pricing
2. regulatory
3. infrastructure and services
4. education
5. marketing.

These help bring about community awareness through participatory urban planning (Burke 1979). The sustainability of the development can be evaluated along with environmental criteria (conservation, green plot ratio, and energy consumption), economic criteria (profitability), and social criteria (social equity and individual satisfaction) over the long term. However, a land use design model (LUDM), as the one proposed in this thesis (the knowledge-based urban development-land use design model [KBUD-LUDM], is incapable of assessing social and economic sustainability (see table 1).

Model *tractability* represents the third arm of the heterogeneity, adaptability, and tractability (HAT) framework. This simply reveals information about the model's internal mechanics (mathematical formulations) that is both necessary for and represented in an understandable or interpretable format to the end user (model intuitiveness). The preparation overload may insist on explaining the database needs, both spatial and tabular formats, along with the programming effort involved in developing the agent-based modelling systems (ABMS) model (Anderson 2002). The agent-based modelling systems (ABMS) can be calibrated using numerical variables (population, jobs, etc.), spatial data sets (land use design zonal maps, GIS), or using block models (3D modelling), and so on. The final model validation takes place in legitimising the behavioural rules that drive the simulation process, which eventually has a critical impact on the overall model's output reliability (Benenson and Torrens 2004).

Table 1. Tabular representation of the heterogeneity, adaptability, and tractability (HAT) framework

Criteria for the HAT agent-based modelling and simulation assessment Benchmarks	
Heterogeneity	
Time	Scalability: duration and step
Space	Abstraction, representation, resolution, and hierarchical variety
Adaptability	
Technical flexibility	Easy integration with other modules (economic, environment assessments, and GIS coupling); output convertibility and case study adaptability [range of model fit]
Policy capability	Pricing; infrastructure and services; regulatory; education/marketing
Tractability	
Intuitiveness	Understandable model (transparent internal mechanics), mathematically tractable (verification)
Preparation workload	Data set availability and extensiveness
Calibration (validation)	Numerical; spatial; behavioural and time
Open source	Algorithms—verifiable and shareable

Source: Adapted version of HAT framework proposed by Ligmann-Zielinska and Jankowski (2007); author (2020).

Secondary Agents

The above-given discussion regarding agent behaviour and the optimisation procedure is restricted to the primary agents—that is, the agents that are the main or anchor tenants of the knowledge-based urban developments (KBUD). However, for the supporting actors (e.g., retail, commercial, recreational, and public spaces), their land uses also play an important role in facilitating a sustainable cluster. In our model, the secondary agents act as supporting actors to the anchor tenants, and these are the additional land uses that the planner would wish to incorporate into the land use design process. As secondary agents are complementary to the primary counterparts, they are often specified as ratios of the former. Planning and design questions relating to how much retail/commercial/recreational/green space should be allotted per person/per hectare/per person within a certain radius (meters) fall into this category.

To perform this task and in the land use design agent-based model, the secondary agents follow three simple rules that are set out on a loop up until the design is optimised for the primary agents in the model (step five in table 10). In their first step, secondary agents are simultaneously created as soon as the primary agents for occupation are declared in the AIP (agent initialisation procedure). Once the primary agents self-locate into land units, secondary agents follow and locate on or the nearest land unit from the primary agent of interest. The users may alternatively set a minimum of x percent gross floor area (GFA) for secondary units in each land unit to allow the secondary agents to support primary agents in every land unit. For example, one can cap retail (food and beverages) space in land units at 10 per cent to allow for mixed-use (vertical) environments. Similar caps on land units may allow for other supporting land uses (residential, recreational, etc.) within the work environment.

Planners would also have urban design goals that stipulate the minimum amount of green space per person, the minimum amount of square foot of the built environment, the minimum amount of retail/commercial/retail spaces to service the resident population—all of which have to be incorporated in the design process. Residential activity also becomes a major aspect of mixed-use developments, and the supporting or service ratios are one way of providing adequate space for such infrastructure. In the one-north case study's initial design conception, these requirements existed throughout the master planning process. For such purposes, in my model, I follow some of the important/necessary planning ratios deployed in the one-north master plan to be consistent with our case study used for subsequent empirical evaluation. For purposes of simplicity, the secondary agents (i.e., green space, commercial/retail, recreational, and housing) are initialised with the following set of minimum requirements. The following minimum planning and data requirement are provided in table 2, and it was used in the one-north's design guidelines. I have used the same in the knowledge-based urban development-land use design model (KBUD-LUDM) for the one-north case study to facilitate the design standardisation purposes. In table 2, the first column shows the housing type of secondary agents, while the second column more specifically states the planning ratios that are to be used in the knowledge-based urban development-land use design model (KBUD-LUDM). These figures are similar to the planning ratios deployed in the one-north master plan (JTC, 2010).

Table 2. Planning ratio assigned for housing in the knowledge-based urban development-land use design simulation model (KBUD-LUDSM)

Type	Planning ratio	Distance
Housing	**Service only 30% of total resident workers**	
Condominiums	1:3 (one unit for every three residents)	Nearest
Semi-detached	1:12 (one unit for every twelve residents)	
Detached	1:6 (one unit for every six residents)	

Source: Adapted from One-North's Design Guidelines (JTC, 2010).

The third column specifies the minimum distance that the agents should be located from the primary agents that they service in the development. At each instance, the secondary agents servicing their primary agents would direct themselves into the nearest land unit with a specific radius that corresponds to its type of service. In the knowledge-based urban development-land use design model (KBUD-LUDM), each retail/commercial or recreational space provided would be nearest from the central position of the primary agent that they are servicing. Previously, I had also mentioned agent allocation process for secondary agents that are not random. Owing to cost considerations, each type of activity has only a finite number of land units that they can use to service the primary agents. The interaction of these two constraints will be an important feature that would give some interesting results. Figure 2 illustrates and summarises the entire land use design simulation process, and the model starts by adopting the agent initialisation procedure (AIP).

Fig. 2. Land use canvas represented by well-defined polylines using Anylogic® simulation program for one-north

Source: JTC (2010); author (2020).

PROJECT MANAGEMENT – AN ARTIFICIAL INTELLIGENT (AI) APPROACH

Table 3. Detailed Land Use Plan for One-North Baseline Scenario

Land Parcel Name	primary Agents	Type of Organisations			Retail	Housing	Total GFA required (sq m)	Footprint (sq m)	Floor Area Ratio (FAR)
		Tech firm (1.1)	University (1.2)	Research institutes (1.3)	Service firms (1.4)				
Biopolis									
BM_3	107	31	11	52	13	27		14,366	2,408	6.00
BM_4	0	-	-	-	-	-	200	2,415	2,318	1.00
BM_5	0	-	-	-	-	-	180	2,174	3,779	0.60
BM_6	92	28	5	50	9	33		12,517	2,036	6.10
Centros	92	37	6	42	7	38		12,527	2,048	6.10
Chromos	73	25	6	36	8	21		9,859	1,646	6.00
Nanos	104	36	11	48	9	18		14,021	2,137	6.60
Genome	76	24	9	37	6	2		10,229	1,692	6.00
Helios	181	55	20	92	14	11		24,407	4,014	6.10
Matrix	115	41	10	56	8	45		15,603	2,553	6.10
Proteos	160	64	12	73	11	-		21,758	3,973	5.50
Total (Biopolis)	1000	339	90	486	85	195	380	142,292	-	-
Fusionopolis									
CX3-5 (fusionopolis)	751	234	75	375	67	56		101,326	9,274	10.90
CX3-4	255	71	24	130	30	15		34,311	7,507	4.60
CX3-1	0						300	3,623	4,315	1.10
CX3-3	-	-	-	-	-	-	150	1,328	1,702	1.06
Total (Fusionopolis)	1006	305	99	505	97	71	410	138,423	-	-

Source: Author (2013, 2020).

NB: Standard setback assumptions are 10 per cent for industrial and 30 per cent of total land for residential land uses.

Table 4. Illustration of the cost array table for one-north utilised for the knowledge-based urban development-land use design model's (KBUD-LUDM) agent environment*

Land parcels	Kb	Area (sq m)	Land use zoning (JTC)	Primary agent access	Development status	Max PR	Conservation status	Green space	Mixed use status	Retail	Residential status
Bm_7	A	4,054	Housing	0	1	4.00	0	0	0	0	1
P1	A	1,693	PARK	0	1	1.00	0	1	0	0	0
OT-5	Sym	1,800	0	1	1	2.00	0	0	0	0	0
Chromos	A	1,828	B park	1	1	4.65	0	0	1	0	0
Genome	A	1,880	B park	1	1	4.65	0	0	1	0	0
P2	A	2,131	PARK	0	1	1.00	0	1	0	0	0
E_6	A	2,220	Inst	1	1	2.90	0	0	0	0	0
Centros	A	2,275	B park	1	1	4.65	0	0	0	0	0
Nanos	A	2,374	B park	1	1	4.65	0	0	1	0	0
W11	Sym	2,662		0	1	4.00	0	0	0	0	0
CX4-7	Sym	2,676		0	1	6.00	0	0	1	0	1
S1	Sym	2,735		0	1	4.00	0	1	0	0	1
BM_3	A	2,776	MU	1	1	5.30	0	0	0	0	0
CX4-2	Sym	2,821	0	1	1	9.00	0	0	0	0	0

Source: Land use zoning data for one-north (JTC [2010]; author [2020]).

NB: A - analytical Kbase; Syn - synthetic Kbase; Sym - symbolic Kbase; B park - business park; Inst - institutional.

*Complete data for all the 150 land parcels would be available on request.

Validation Procedure

The rise of models in the agent-based modelling (ABM) literature has led to an increased awareness amongst modellers to check and correct for path dependency and multiple equilibrium issues especially in economic, ecological, and spatial land use systems (Atkinson and Oleson 1996; Balmann 2001; Pahl-Wostl 1995). Path dependency arises from negative and positive feedback that reinforce on each other to create large deviations from the optimal results. Thus, there is an increased necessity to validate spatial land use models. Multiple equilibria are unfavourable as they increase model's uncertainty in obtaining land use design solutions for planning purposes. One can extend these concerns to our model, which is a land use design optimisation model. To get around this problem, D. G. Brown et al. (2005) suggest that modellers focus on two aspects to validate agent-based land use models. The first is by employing *aggregate similarity* followed by *spatial similarity*.

Aggregate similarity is used to refer to similarities in statistical terms, whereby the mapped pattern of land use design is in line with the functional relationships specified in the model. In other land use agent-based models, this could be statistics that describe either the size of developed clusters, the relationship between distance to city centre, global density, or any other standardised performance measurements (Batty and Longley 1994; Makse, Andrade, Batty, Havlin, and Stanley 1998). The knowledge-based urban development-land use design model (KBUD-LUDM) for one-north generates optimised land use designs for a given design criteria along with a set of rational assumptions (see table 5). Thus, the *aggregate similarity* validation procedure would be able to test the robustness of the

KBUD-LUDM's ability to generate optimal designs for varying inputs measured by the global parameters (∂_G & σ_G) for a variety of inputs and assumptions.

The performance of the global parameter Delta (∂_G)/Sigma (σ_G) obtained through the model using equations (7) and (8) is used to evaluate the design outcomes for a given increasing set of agents and varying assumptions (see sets A–E in table 5).

This would act as a stress test to determine the robustness of the agent-based model to handle a variety of planning situations if the need arises. Table 5 shows the aggregate validation procedure performed for the knowledge-based urban development-land use design model (KBUD-LUDM) for the case study of one-north. Here, the first column (number of simulations) represents several rounds of stress tests using a set of initialisation parameters and assumptions, which are given in table 5.

Table 0. List of varying assumption sets for the empirical validation procedure of the KBUD-LUDM

Assumption Set	Number of agents	Agent characteristics		
		Knowledge base	Organisational	Institutional (Public-Private ratio)
A (Baseline)	2,000	α=0.5, β=0.5, γ=0	TF=0.30, RI=0.50, EI=0.10, SF=0.10	80:20
B	3,000	α=0.3, β=0.4, γ=0.3	TF=0.10, RI=0.40, EI=0.20, SF=0.30	70:30
C	4,000	α=0.2, β=0.3, γ=0.5	TF=0.60, RI=0.10, EI=0.10, SF=0.20	60:40
D	5,000	α=0.35, β=0.1, γ=0.6	TF=0.10, RI=0.80, EI=0.05, SF=0.05	40:60
E	6,000	α=0.1, β=0.8, γ=0.1	TF=0.15, RI=0.10, EI=0.10, SF=0.65	20:80

NB: The agent's characteristics in table 5.11 are assigned randomly such that extreme values make a representative case to stress the model's performance.

The second column of table 5 shows the total number of agents initialised, whereas the third column gives the output of the global parameters—Delta (∂_G)/Sigma (σ_G) after the first round of simulation. Results in table 5 show the *aggregate* or empirical validation of the knowledge-based urban development-land use design model (KBUD-LUDM) developed for one-north knowledge-based urban development (KBUD). The target for the global parameters (column 5) has been set with a 20 per cent deviation window.[10] The optimal value for ∂_G is 0.5 according to the previously proposed knowledge interaction design criteria (KIDC) with a window of 30 per cent standard deviation.

Column 7 in table 5 tells us the model for a set of assumptions (N), number of agents (x), at the nth simulation trial, whether the global parameter is satisfied or not. If the answer is a 'yes', then the knowledge-based urban development-land use design model (KBUD-LUDM) exports the design outcome as the final solution at every stage. To check for consistency of the results from the knowledge-based urban development-land use design model (KBUD-LUDM), the validation procedure can be performed for different combinations of 'actors' as shown in table 5. A robust model should be able to deliver optimal solutions for different sets of agents and assumptions.

The results do show that the KBUD-LUDM is able to handle multiple inputs and varying assumptions. For every set of assumption, the last column in table 5.9 shows the solution of an optimum design at the nth trial where the global evaluation parameter delta's mean and deviation is considerably close to the optimal value. The optimal design solution for the last scenario (set E), however, is unattainable. This was shown as an 'overstack' error with JAVA—that is, one of the constraints adopted early on was too rigid.

---

[10] As previously mentioned, the deviation window can be tightened or relaxed by the user. Ideally in a 'continuous' environment, this would not be necessary; however, in a constrained environment, optimal solutions are difficult to obtain. To get around this problem, I use a small deviation window. Theoretically, this does not challenge my design outcome as I previously claim the maximum interactive designs can be achieved within the 'optimal window'(∂), figure 14, which leaves room for slight deviations from the norm.

Table 6. Hypothetical example of the 'aggregate validation' procedure used for the knowledge-based urban development-land use design model (KBUD-LUDM)

Assumptions (as given in Table 5.10)	Number of agents	Cumulative agents in KBUD system	Global Delta (∂_G)	Target ∂ $\partial_G \sim 0.50$	Standard deviation σ_G	Optimal design solution (Yes or NO)
Set A (baseline scenario)	2,000	2,000	$\partial_{TF}=0.70, \partial_{RI}=0.10$ $\partial_{EI}=0.10, \partial_{I}=0.10$	$\partial_G=.31$	0.26	Yes
Set B	3,000	5,000	$\partial_{TF}=0.70, \partial_{RI}=0.10$ $\partial_{EI}=0.10, \partial_{I}=0.10$	$\partial_G=0.43$	0.23	Yes
Set C	4,000	9,000	$\partial_{TF}=0.70, \partial_{RI}=0.10$ $\partial_{EI}=0.10, \partial_{I}=0.10$	$\partial_G=0.35$	0.22	Yes
Set D	5,000	14,000	$\partial_{TF}=0.70, \partial_{RI}=0.10$ $\partial_{EI}=0.10, \partial_{I}=0.10$	$\partial_G\sim0.59$	0.37	yes
Set E	6,000	20,000	$\partial_{TF}=0.70, \partial_{RI}=0.10$ $\partial_{EI}=0.10, \partial_{I}=0.10$	NA	NA	NO

Source: Author (2020).

The function of the cost matrix is to restrict primary and secondary agents to specific land parcels to maintain development costs. In this case, some of the secondary agents were found not to have space for allocation (refer to the cost matrix given in table 6). As secondary agents could not be satisfied, the loop was terminated, resulting in an error. However, this is not to suggest that the framework is inefficient, but, rather, our cost constraints for the one-north case study is stringent. This may be corrected by changing the fundamental assumptions of the planning ratios or the cost matrix to favour more secondary agents in the environment by enabling a more generous zoning to those actors.

The second type of validation is *spatial similarity* advocated in the literature (D. G. Brown et al. 2005), which refers to the degree of match between existing land use maps and those generated using single or multiple runs of the subject agent-based model. The validation would entail a direct comparison between land use designs (existing versus generated). In my thesis, I employ a two-tier visual validation procedure—the first being two-dimensional simulated outputs generated using agent-based modelling (ABM). The two-dimensional model is extrapolated into the three-dimensional block models to conduct a visual inspection against the existing block structures at one-north. Recall that there are several advantages of having a three-dimensional arm to a land use design model. The baseline validation procedure has performed the spatial similarity validation procedure. The baseline scenario shows the three-dimensional block diagram output from CityCAD® from the knowledge-based urban development-land use design model (KBUD-LUDM) agent-based model. However, this is by no means fully comparable to the built environment at one-north because complete path dependency for validation is not realistically achievable by the KBUD-LUDM, as it is not a predictive agent-based model.

In a predictive agent-based model, the modeller often needs to answer the following question, 'Can the model predict past behaviour?' In the KBUD-LUDM, one can approximately replicate the physical mould of one-north at every stage of development, but existing land use design details (mixed-use ratios) are hard to replicate for two reasons. First, in the KBUD-LUDM, the physical moulds (plot ratio and GFA) are achieved through the allocation of actors on-site using the scientific principle of the knowledge interaction design criteria (KIDC), which was not the case for the land use design exhibited in the master plans. Second, even if mixed-use design ratios could be replicated, tenant data regarding current mixed-use design ratio at one-north is unavailable for purposes of comparison.

Nevertheless, the aim of this thesis is not to propose a land use design model to replace existing master planning techniques but to enhance it to provide a more detailed and targeted and, most importantly, incremental[11] land use design planning approach for knowledge-based urban developments (KBUDs). Traditional

---

[11] Incremental planning could be thought of a slow approach to urban planning and design rather than a one-shot completely top-down approach. Incremental planning is thus a more flexible option especially for large-scale projects with high uncertainty levels (Batty et al. 2000).

urban planning through master planning techniques has a top-down approach, where the physical planning informs current levels of *activity* on-site. Such approach is a more 'hardware' approach to modern industrial development, wherein physical planning is conducted without due consideration of the probable interrelationship between actors on the KBUD sites.

For large-scale post-industrial clusters such as one-north, given a set of actors, the KBUD-LUDM will facilitate urban planners to first achieve the right 'software' to enhance intra-cluster interactions between related actors and then upon which determine the space required to facilitate them through mixed-use zoning ratios (physical planning). Overall, this section concludes the empirical or aggregate validation procedure as advocated by D. G. Brown et al. (2005) for agent-based land use models.

The Labels Utilised

ZD	zonal division
LUCC	land use cost criteria
TLPA	total land parcel area
PR	plot ratio
SPA	space per agent (in meters)
Mnop	minimum number of persons
MSRPP	minimum space required per person
PRcap$_{li}$	plot ratio cap for land unit l_i
FAR	floor area ratio
∂_G	global delta value for a land use design output (evaluation criteria)
σ_G	global sigma value for a land use design output (evaluation criteria)
KIDC	knowledge interaction design criteria
DUPM	dynamic urban planning methodology
TF	technology firm

RI	research institution
EI	educational institution
SF	service firm
Kb	knowledge base
Ob	organisational base
Ib	institutional base
Cb	cognitive base
α	analytical knowledge base (in percentage)
β	synthetic knowledge base (in percentage)
γ	symbolic knowledge base (in percentage)

CHAPTER 7

THE CONCLUSION

On the whole, this book has essentially offered useful insights into the influential factors and operational scenarios, key assumptions, and limitations of an ensuing model. The book is a unique and novel treatment of project management from artificial intelligence that entails data analytics, deploying neural networks, fuzzy logic, genetic algorithm(s); and data visualisation, deploying agent-based modelling (ABM) in, for instance, the knowledge-based urban development (KBUD). The book discusses the discipline of project management in modern light and how it can be competently adopted by design engineers, urban planners, project managers, quantity and real estate surveyors, public and private real estate developers, architects for new and existing developments, as well as scholars.

Neural networks represent a state-of-the-art approach that intelligently searches for underlying relationships amongst the time series concerned through adapting or changing the connection weights that represent the array of variables, thereby overcoming the problems associated with sharp corrections, and the paucity and non-stationarity of the data. Unlike the traditional statistical method, which needs a priori parametric knowledge of the form of linear or non-linear function to be tested, neural networks do not need such information beforehand to predict the future possible outcomes. The neural networks are designed to capture the non-linear relationship between the input and output variables automatically. They are useful for solving complex problems that are too difficult to apply constrained-optimisation algorithm. A creative, flexible solution can be 'invented' through neural networks.

Chapter 1 demonstrates the estimating of construction demand via the use of neural network models to predict the output factor, the value of contracts awarded. The results seem to suggest that the RNN/DRS has the best trainability network for the period 1981 to 1996. However, the MNN and FBP networks are still able to offer reasonably good explanatory strength towards the prediction of the level and pattern of construction demand. Neural networks offer a realistic measure of construction demand, which is necessary if effective effort is to be made to maintain, and improve upon, the capacity of the industry. They can also advise on how to moderate the swings in construction outputs through various measures such as monetary and fiscal policies.

Chapter 2 reiterates that new private office and residential supply like in Hong Kong (HK) depends on current prices returned by the market relative to the cost of replacing or building them. In the long run, the market should equate market-clearing prices with replacement costs, which include the cost of land. In the short run, however, the two may diverge significantly because of the lags and delays inherent to the building process. Apart from these real estate cyclical factors, land use policies and control mechanisms—for example, the Land Sales Program of the Urban Redevelopment Authority (URA) in Singapore—also plays a role in stabilising new real estate supply and prices.

Rent is a key decision factor, and the demand for existing/new space depends on rent and factors such as income levels, firm's production levels, and number of households. New supply and demand are also affected by fluctuations in the cost of borrowing and induced changes related to the national income. Private residential demand is influenced by the government's budgetary policy in the building programme of the public housing substitute sector and by the cost of credit and the availability of money administered by the Monetary Authority of Singapore (MAS). Increasing money supply and lowering of credit cost stimulate more investment demand for real estate. Fiscal policy involving changes in tax and subsidies can also affect the rate of real estate development. In this chapter, the NNGA model can be readily adopted to develop the outlooks for the prime HK Office sector.

Chapter 3 discusses the specific tasks to be planned to include the following:

- develop life cycle models and metrics for analysing each technology/innovation. This includes extending the application of the LCA to Consequential LCA.
- compare relative life cycle sustainability performance of each technology/innovation;
- conduct systems integration of most promising technologies/innovations;
- develop scenarios for the deployment of technologies/innovations including rates of penetration and develop business-as-usual scenarios for comparison;
- develop resiliency perturbation scenarios and model system responses;
- characterise uncertainties and trade-offs between meeting sustainability and resiliency objectives, and prioritise technology and design options;
- characterise interconnectedness of system components and develop network models to simulate system responses to internal and external challenges, including consequence analysis as a kind of network modelling. The network, in this case, can be revealed using a technique known as 'technology ecosystem analysis'.
- development of energy resilience model for a number of key building types using the total building performance (TBP) approach;

- develop energy resilience score matrix and under empirical studies to ascertain energy resilience index for different building systems and performance mandates;
- apply the system dynamic modelling method to test the response and behaviour of the energy resilience model using scenario approach;
- assess the contributions of each technology and innovation to national energy policy goals.

Chapter 4 draws attention to the trend that in a highly volatile world, the best point estimate of the classical DCF model is no longer a reliable indication of the investment worth. The investment evaluation becomes outdated or obsolete rapidly as the state of the direct real estate market (DREM) changes. Many sophisticated forecasting techniques have been proposed and advanced to consolidate the variances. These techniques are criticised for generating inconsistent outcomes when the DREM is not so a random walk. Therefore, the expert experiences and market knowledge appear to be better substitutes for those quantitative methodologies in an attempt to outguess the DREM performance. The translation of these expert experiences and judgements into reliable market forecasts suffers from some limitations. Imprecision and vagueness are major obstacles to the application of expert knowledge. Incorporation of fuzzy set theory to the classical models is proposed as a way to overcome the problems of fuzziness.

The fuzzy DCF model provides a natural and intuitive way of dealing with cognitive uncertainty. It relaxes the precision and crispness imposed on a rigid model, for an inexact and vague but robust representation of DREM knowledge. Investors and analysts are consequently not restrained to make imprecise but reliable predictions and relieving them of adopting data-intensive statistical analyses. Based on a set of fuzzy inputs, the fuzzy NPV can be imputed to provide an approximated evaluation of the investment interest. With the membership characteristics of the fuzzy NPVs, the uncertainty of each outcome is concurrently captured and reflected.

Such a fuzzy NPV approximative model merges two limbs of investment analysis—the return and risk evaluation.

In the case illustrations, the NPV of the classical DCF model based on crisp and precise inputs is estimated at S$5,563,288. When the input variables are fuzzified with different possibility distributions, the fuzzy NPV post the centroid defuzzification process gives an optimal value of S$8,532,785. A comparison of the results shows that an increase in NPV of 53.38 per cent is obtained by the fuzzy DCF vis-à-vis the classical NPV. The implication is the assumption of greater uncertainties in the fuzzy DCF analysis. The gap between the fuzzy DCF and the classical NPV is partly attributable to the trade-off in generalising the classical model and the assumption of uncertainty. However, the gap also reflects a higher degree of optimism in the transformation of approximate estimates to the respective fuzzy numbers. Cognitive uncertainty has long been overlooked in the past. As the DREM moves away from randomness, the ability to deal with this form of uncertainty ultimately distinguishes the more viable and savvy investors. The application of the fuzzy DCF offers a competitive edge to the enlightened investor.

Chapter 5 discusses the fuzzy tactical asset allocation (FTAA) model, which incorporates intuitive decision-making into the asset allocation process from the perspective of the expert investor (decision maker). This FTAA model can improve the efficiency of asset allocation, adopting fuzzy set theory and fuzzy optimisation theory. The FTAA model portfolios both show more positive allocations relative to the MPT TAA model portfolio, which have more 0 per cent allocation weights, reflecting intuitively greater Asian city diversification in the short run. In terms of portfolio risk minimisation, the FTAA robust programming model is as good as the MPT TAA model portfolio from table 11. All three TAA models are able to achieve optimal risk-adjusted returns at the portfolio level. Both the Zimmerman FTAA flexible programming model and the Ramik and Rimanek FTAA robust programming model have higher portfolio risk each, given the same portfolio return. It is attributable to these two FTAA models that intuitively incorporate more risk each from the investor's perspective, relative to the MPT TAA model.

In contrast, the quadratic programming optimisation of the MPT TAA model incorporates the risk minimisation objective that is strictly observed, and any violation of its constraints is unacceptable regardless of the extent of noncompliance. Such a rigid approach conflicts with the real-world problem, where the investor and asset project manager may not insist on minimum risk but rather desire a more tolerable level of risk. Consequently, a small violation of the constraints within the tolerance interval should not cause the investor and asset project manager decision maker to reject the feasible solution.

The MPT TAA model is essentially a quadratic programming optimisation model that is highly sensitive to estimation errors. Therefore, the precision and reliability of its estimated inputs are critical to the success of the optimisation decision. Determination of input variables relies on historical data, which is proven to be increasingly unreliable for forecasting purposes, in view of the refutation of the random walk hypothesis in the common stock and direct real estate markets. Expert investors with good market knowledge can provide reasonable estimates of returns, thereby relinquishing the reliance on data-intensive statistical approaches. Nevertheless, investor's and asset project manager's judgements are each constrained by the fact that the confidence of their judgements can be improved only at the expense of precision. This form of uncertainty, which is attributed to the vagueness of information and imprecision, can be quantified by fuzzy set theory.

Incorporating fuzzy set theory with the quadratic programming model offers investment and asset project management allocators with the more intuitive and natural way of capturing expert investor judgement in asset optimisation, in particular for international direct real estate portfolio allocation on a risk-adjusted basis. Both the Zimmerman FTAA flexible programming model and the Ramik and Rimanek FTAA robust programming model to asset optimisation are equally good alternatives relative to the MPT TAA model. Such two

FTAA models achieve the twofold benefits of intuitively greater risk diversification by city or real estate sector and enable effective risk management. It is anticipated that these two short-run FTAA fuzzy models are expected to be readily accepted, and more such models are emerging as the effective extension of quadratic programming optimisation as more computable software programs of this kind become widespread.

Fuzzy approaches to optimisation for asset allocation in the short run have a limitation. In general, the fuzzy model exhibits the common feature of converting the equality function under quadratic programming optimisation into inequality functions. Such inequality optimisation replaces the point solution of the MPT TAA optimisation problem (owing to the latter's rigid intersection of all functions), with a generalised or intuitive answer over a defined space of alternatives. The product of the fuzzy process with fuzzy inputs, in the form of the fuzzy outcome, is, in actual fact, a more natural and intuitive approach to investment and asset project management optimisation.

Last, chapter 6 reiterates that city planners of the twenty-first century see the knowledge-based urban development (KBUD) strategy as a new form of urban renewal of industrial cities. The planners believe it can potentially bring economic, technological progress, and sustainable socio-spatial order to the contemporary city.[24] Inefficient large-scale urban designs of planned post-industrial complexes clusters have the potential to create dissociation of related activities. This resulting rise of physical barriers can lead to a reduced level of intra-cluster knowledge interactions via both planned and spontaneous channels.

Chapter 6 addresses the growing need for an urban design criterion that aid in efficient land use planning for knowledge-based urban developments (KBUDs). Apart from aesthetic benefits, the chapter discusses that planned mixed-use land use designs can help shape knowledge interactions between different types of actors by placing 'related' workers together. By exploring the literature on knowledge interactions and their determinants between different actors, one can first develop a unique urban design criterion, which is aimed at enhancing knowledge interactions (KIs) in the knowledge-based urban developments (KBUDs). This chapter defines 'actors' in the KBUDs in terms of their specific roles in the KBUD innovation ecosystem. Then drawing on important discussions from the innovation and proximity dynamics literature, one can propose what is known as the knowledge interaction design criteria (KIDC) to help urban planners associate related actors together in space. Having such a criteria satisfies one of the three important rationales stated by urban planners when performing land use zoning—that is, to integrate compatible land uses, to generate positive externalities, and to achieve mutual benefit.

A formal representation of a knowledge-based urban development-land use design model (KBUD-LUDM) incorporating the knowledge interaction design criteria (KIDC) is proposed, adopting agent-based methodology to obtain optimal land use design solutions. Agent-based approach is an alternative methodology to handle spatial and temporal processes, compared to the linear programming methodology, which has been used to address land use design problems.

The agent-based approach, which addresses the KBUDs, is meant to be an incremental planning approach to save time and resources in redesigning/rezoning efforts, under uncertain economic conditions. Promoting intra-cluster interactions by co-agglomerating knowledge-intensive actors and adopting better mixed-use zoning strategies can improve the attractiveness of the specialised direct real estate like the KBUD project in the marketplace.

ENDNOTES

1. OECD (2000).
2. Storper (1992); Cesaroni and Piccaluga (2003).
3. With the exception of Allen (1984); Toker and Gray (2008).
4. See for city branding.
5. In this chapter 6, urban design criteria refer more specifically to the land use design criteria that determine the spatial allocation of activities.
6. A characteristic feature of workers in knowledge-based industries.
7. Urban precinct here is defined as an election district of a city or town.
8. http://www.urbandesign.org/
9. These interactions can be social (by aggregating residential land uses), economic (establishing business clusters), environmental (providing access to green space, conservation), and so on.
10. http://www.urbandesign.gov.au/whatis/index.aspx
11. Actors who belong to a common economic, institutional, or organisational entity.
12. An example of regional agglomeration would be the 'Blue Banana' in Western Europe. The financial centres in the city of London and advertising industry at 'Madison Avenue' in New York are good examples of industrial agglomeration on a metropolitan and neighbourhood level.
13. The word 'actor' here in this context is used to refer to knowledge workers who participate in knowledge-based clusters.
14. See Asheim and Gertler (2005) for a detailed discussion.
15. This is equivalent to reducing the average geographical distance between actors in the knowledge-based urban development (KBUD).
16. Bounded rationality is the idea that in decision-making, rationality of individuals is limited by the information they have, the cognitive limitations of their minds, and the finite amount of time they have to make a decision.
17. Note: The organisational proximity refers to both inter-organisation and intra-organisational proximity between agents.

18. Apart from the most common subsidiary land uses, for a knowledge-based development, this could be more specific amenities such as seminar rooms, libraries, cafes, restaurants, and so on.
19. Optimisation is given in equation (1).
20. http://www.a-star.edu.sg/Biopolis-Fusionopolis/A-Vision-for-Convergence/Fusionopolis.aspx
21. http://www.ascendas.com/images_common/cms/press_release/137/Press release_-_First_Building_at_Mediapolis_11Feb2011.pdf
22. See Lee et al. (2008); Yigitcanlar, O'Connor, et al. (2008).
23. While the other two rationales are (2) separating incompatible uses that generate negative externalities; and (3) interjecting public goods like roads and open space to improve social welfare (environmental benefits).

www.ingramcontent.com/pod-product-compliance
Lightning Source LLC
Chambersburg PA
CBHW030929180526
45163CB00002B/510